CONSTABLE OIL SKETCHES

JOHN BASKETT

Constable Oil Sketches

BARRIE & JENKINS
COMMUNICA - EUROPA

© 1966 BY JOHN BASKETT
FIRST PUBLISHED 1966 BY
BARRIE & ROCKLIFF (BARRIE BOOKS LTD.)
THIRD IMPRESSION 1972
FOURTH IMPRESSION 1975
PUBLISHED BY BARRIE & JENKINS LTD
24 HIGHBURY CRESCENT, LONDON N5 1RX
ALL RIGHTS RESERVED
NO PART OF THIS PUBLICATION MAY BE REPRODUCED IN ANY FORM
OR BY ANY MEANS WITHOUT PRIOR PERMISSION OF BARRIE & JENKINS LTD.
PHOTOGRAPHS (EXCEPT FOR NUMBER 14) BY
RODNEY TODD-WHITE, LONDON
TYPESET IN MONOTYPE BASKERVILLE BY
V. SIVITER SMITH & CO. LTD., BIRMINGHAM
PRINTED AND BOUND IN GT. BRITAIN
BY W. S. COWELL LTD., IPSWICH
ISBN 0 214 16029 7

IN SOME WAYS CONSTABLE'S OIL SKETCHES are the surest guide to his artistic and spiritual struggle for self-expression. Most of them were painted on the spot under the direct inspiration of nature. They transmit strong power of suggestion, because they have captured and preserved what were essentially passing manifestations of nature, and changing effects of light. In these small works, Constable's genius enabled him to avoid the pitfalls of emotional involvement on the one hand, and on the other of dry literalness. Being relatively small, they did not present the problems of handling paint over a large area, with its attendant risks of losing immediacy. Although a few were used as studies for large-scale works, and others as subjects to be engraved in the *English Landscape* series, there were, by and large, painted in the first place for the artist's own pleasure and instruction.

Constable usually sketched before his subject with a painting box resting on his knees. Occasionally he worked from the windows of houses where he was living. He painted quickly, (No. 15, *Study of Sky and Trees at Hampstead,* was completed in an hour), and his talent demanded a technique which would by-pass the slow processes of studio painting, entirely reliant as they were on pencil studies and a good visual memory. The solution lay in using spirit colours on paper. Nineteen of the sketches reproduced here were painted in this way. The great virtue of paper, apart from its portability, was that, properly sized, it was less absorbant than a gesso ground, and by using quick-drying spirit colours a sketch could be completed at one sitting. The absence of linseed oil in the medium resulted in some 'flatness', but the sketches largely revived on being varnished. The innovation did not lie so much in the technique itself as in the manner in which Constable used it. Examples of painting in oil on paper can be found on the Continent as early as the sixteenth century, but Constable appears to have been the first to fully exploit its possibilities for rapid sketching from nature. It is not clear where he learned the technique, although his friend and mentor, Sir George Beaumont is known to have tried his hand at it. Beaumont may have adopted the idea from Richard Wilson's pupil, Thomas Jones (1743-1803), whose oil sketches made in and around Naples must have been familiar to him. Another characteristic of Constable's sketching technique was his habit of toning his working surface in advance. In this way he avoided the time-consuming business of 'blocking in', in order to obliterate the white background before applying local colour.

All the plates in the present anthology may truthfully be described as sketches with the possible exceptions of No. 13, *Dedham Vale with Ploughman* and No. 32, *A View of London with Sir Richard Steele's Cottage,* both of which must have been entirely executed in the studio. They are selected from two of the finest and most comprehensive collections of Constable's sketches. That at the Victoria and Albert Museum, from which twenty-four examples have been chosen, has been in existence there for over seventy-five years, and derives from the gift of the artist's second daughter, Isabel Constable, who died in 1888. Many of these sketches had been bought in bundles by the family at the artist's sale in 1838 for less than the small reserve prices, and it was only fifty years later, when they were exhibited at South Kensington, that the eyes of the public were opened to the special qualities of this side of Constable's art. Apart from drawings and watercolours, Miss Constable gave and bequeathed ninety-five paintings to the Museum.

Eight of the forty or so Constable sketches in the collection formed by Mr. and Mrs. Paul Mellon of Upperville, Virginia, are reproduced here. The sketches are only part, albeit an important part, of a much larger collection of English pictures assembled in recent years by Mr. and Mrs. Mellon.

John Constable was born at East Bergholt, Suffolk, on the 11th June 1776. He was the second son of Golding Constable, a prosperous mill-owner and of his wife Ann. Constable's father, although he had known difficult times, was a successful merchant. He owned watermills at Dedham and Flatford, and a windmill and a roundhouse near East Bergholt, but his function was one of merchant and supervisor rather than miller. His success led him to build a substantial Georgian house next to the church at East Bergholt, and it was here that the artist was born.

It was feared that Constable would die in infancy, but he survived and at the age of seven was sent to boarding school. He later removed to a school at Lavenham, and again to the Rev. Dr. Grimwood's grammar school at Dedham. He had lessons from a tutor in French, but we learn from his friend, Archdeacon Fisher, at the time of his success in Paris in 1824, that he couldn't speak a word of the language. There appears at first to have been some hope on the part of his parents that he would enter the church, but he had remarkably little aptitude for scholarship, and Leslie's kind, urbane biography effectively disguises the fact that, despite his attractive and fresh style of letter writing, he wasn't particularly literate. Shortly after he left school and had gone on a visit to Edmonton, he wrote to his father, "I found that I deserved all the reproof you was so good as to give me; and moreover I should not think you was my friend if you did not give it when you see it is necessary as it certainly then was".

6

On leaving school, Constable was set to work for a year in his father's mills, the intention being that he should train in the family business with a view to carrying it on. From childhood, however, he had an intense love of his natural surroundings, although his resolve to become a painter would appear to have been something which only established itself by stages. He wrote in later years, "The sound of water escaping from mill-dams, etc., willows, old rotten planks, slimy posts and brickwork – I love such things. Painting is with me but another word for feeling, and I associate my 'careless boyhood' with all that lies on the banks of the Stour. Those scenes made me a painter and I am grateful – that is, I had often thought of pictures before I ever touched a pencil".

In his youth Constable formed an association with an artisan from the village called John Dunthorne (1770-1844). This man was an enthusiastic amateur painter and the two joined forces, renting a little building in East Bergholt as a studio and going off on sketching expeditions together. Another friendship developed when Constable was sent to Edmonton in 1796 to visit an uncle. This time it was with the artist J. T. Smith (1766-1833), who was then working as a drawing master. 'Antiquity' Smith, as he came to be known, because of his publications on old London, was appointed Keeper of Prints and Drawings at the British Museum in 1816. He is perhaps best remembered today as the witty author of *Book for a Rainy Day* and of *Nollekens and his Times*. Smith's attachment to picturesque, tumbledown cottages led Constable, under his influence, to make a few feeble drawings of dilapidated cottages and to attempt, unsuccessfully, to learn the technique of etching. By far the most important contact, however, of his early youth was his meeting with Sir George Beaumont. Ann Constable, who was acquainted with the dowager Lady Beaumont, residing at that time at Dedham, was able to effect an introduction for her son while Sir George was in the neighbourhood visiting his mother. The friendship that developed between these two men, divided by class, age and temperament, lasted until Sir George's death. Sir George Beaumont (1753-1827) appears to have been a man whose refined ecclecticism imbued his patronage with strong preferences and pre-conceived ideas. Despite his somewhat rigid manner, (he addressed people with Johnsonean phraseology, and his visual experiences took place through a Claude-glass), he was essentially a warm-hearted, spontaneous extrovert. A measure of the excellence of his taste was that his Old Master paintings helped form, with the Angerstein pictures, the nucleus of the National Collection. But Beaumont also possessed works by recent and contemporary artists, notably J. R. Cozens, and Thomas Girtin. He was no mean performer himself, and evolved a quite distinct style of his own. In his youth he had taken lessons from Richard Wilson.

The fundamental difference in outlook between Beaumont and Constable was that the latter only permitted nature to be his real master. In the lecture delivered at the Hampstead Assembly Rooms in 1833, towards the end of his life, Constable says of eighteenth century landscape art "–the painters of this period added nothing to the general stock, as their predecessors had done by original study, but referring always to the pictures of their masters instead of looking to the aspects of nature which had given birth to those pictures." He goes on to exempt from this criticism the work of Wilson, Gainsborough, Cozens and Girtin. Beaumont's axiom, vestigious from the eighteenth century, but still widely upheld at that time, that it was essential to give a warm yellow tonality to a picture, similar to the effect produced by age and a discoloured varnish, was unacceptable to Constable. Constable's technique, nevertheless, was throughout his life firmly rooted in the Old Masters, and his habit of painting on a toned ground and applying opaque white pigment to produce the highlights; his rich colour harmonies and his brilliant ability to produce atmosphere from the effects of light, derive from Ruysdael, Rubens and Claude. It was primarily through Beaumont's friendship and generosity that he was able to study and discuss these artists.

In March 1797 Constable wrote to J. T. Smith "I must now take your advice and attend my father's business–I see plainly it will be my lot to walk through life in a path contrary to that in which my inclination would lead me." We are led to assume that Smith had discouraged Constable from embarking on a financially hazardous profession when enthusiasm appeared to be his only qualification, and when a sound family business offered a secure alternative. Smith was echoing the feelings of Constable's mother and father, yet they must have been an indulgent couple, for two years later, in March 1799, he was admitted to the Academy Schools on the recommendation of Joseph Farington,

and was enrolled as a student in February of the following year.

The first decade of the nineteenth century saw Constable pursuing a number of false trails. His family were hoping that he would turn to portrait painting, because of the greater financial security it offered, and on this score they obtained for him commissions to make portraits of some of the farmers and their wives in the vicinity of East Bergholt. He painted a rather feeble altarpiece in the manner of West for the church at Brantham, and a somewhat better one for Nayland Church. The copies he made for Lord Dysart of family portraits by Reynolds and Hoppner probably improved his technique, but portrait painting was never his strong point, although he was at his best when painting the faces of his family or of those with whom he felt intimate ties.

During this period Constable was slowly finding himself in his landscape painting. As early as 1802 he announced his *credo* in a letter to John Dunthorne. "For the last two years", he says, "I have been running after pictures, and seeking the truth at second hand. I have not endeavoured to represent nature with the same elevation of mind with which I set out, but rather tried to make my performances look like the work of other men. I am come to a determination to make no idle visits this summer, nor to give up my time to commonplace people. I shall return to Bergholt, where I shall endeavour to get a pure and unaffected manner of representing the scenes that may employ me. There is little or nothing in the exhibition worth looking up to. *There is room enough for a natural painture. The great vice of the present day is bravura, an attempt to do something beyond the truth." The landscape sketches of 1802, mostly of thickly wood scenery in Dedham Vale, show a marked advance on Constable's earliest work. The tones are predominantly green and brown, and although one is vaguely left with the feeling that he has been looking over his shoulder at the prints of Anthonie Waterloo, there is no evidence of his having worked to a pre-conceived formula. His close observation of nature in these studies, particularly of the effect of light, led the perceptive and sympathetic West to remark when looking at one, "You must have loved nature very much before you could have painted this."

Constable visited the Lake District in the Autumn of 1806. It isn't known why he undertook the journey, but it may well have been at the suggestion of Sir George Beaumont. Lakeland scenery provided the nearest equivalent to be found in England to the type of Italian landscape which such artists as Claude and Richard Wilson had painted. Even if Constable had wished to visit Italy, which is doubtful, the journey would have been ruled out not only on financial grounds, but also by virtue of the Napoleonic Wars which for most of the period rendered Continental travel extremely difficult, if not out of the question. In 1823 he writes chauvinistically, "I am doomed never to see the living scenes that inspired the landscape of Wilson and Claude. No, but I was born to paint a happier land, my own dear old England." The legacy of Constable's two months in the Lake District comprises a number of broadly washed but muddy watercolour drawings, and a few paintings, which show a good grasp of drawing, although they are rather harshly coloured. On the back of one of the drawings from the series he has written "25 Sepr. 1805 (for 1806) – Borrowdale – fine clouday day tone very mellow like – the mildest of Gaspar Poussin and Sir G(eorge) B(eaumont) and on the whole deeper toned than this drawing." There is no doubt that what Constable meant to say was that certain paintings by Gaspar and Sir George produced an effect similar to the landscape he saw, rather than that the landscape looked like their pictures. It was Beaumont who saw finished 'picturesque' landscapes through the eyes of other artists.

By dint of exertion, exploring every avenue, and working all the time to develop a natural technique of his own, Constable ended the first decade of the century in a sense where he had started it, but on another level. In 1799, when he was made a probationer at the Academy Schools, he was fresh from an isolated country village and virtually without any training. By 1810, at the age of thirty-four, he knew with certainty in what direction he wanted to develop his art, and by that time he had the technical resources and method to accomplish his aim. His was no sudden arrival, and later in life he wrote to his friend Fisher, "I imagine myself driving a nail. I have driven it some way – by persevering with this nail I may drive it home."

The next few years produced a rich output of oil sketches. Constable was spending more and more time during the summer months at East Bergholt, and the first ten plates in this anthology, and the original of No. 13, dating from 1811 to c. 1815, were probably all made in the

vicinity of his birthplace. The scene of the *Village Fair at East Bergholt* (plate 1) appears to have been sketched from a window in his father's house, and the other two identifiable views from this group, *Barges on the Stour* (plate 2) and *East Bergholt Church* (plate 3) are within a stone's throw of the same spot. Subjects must have presented themselves to Constable at every turn. In the Victoria and Albert Museum, there are two sketchbooks, small in dimension and dating from the years 1813 and 1814, which he filled with precious little thumbnail sketches of the local scenery. Some of the work done at this period was to act as a storehouse of imagery which Constable drew from to furnish pictures painted later in his career. The *Autumnal Sunset* of c. 1812 (plate 6) served as one of the subjects for the *English Landscape* series, being engraved by David Lucas and published in the fifth number in 1832.

1811 had been a promising year for Constable. In the autumn, Bishop Fisher and his wife invited him to Salisbury to spend three weeks with them at the Palace. It was here that he met the Bishop's nephew, John Fisher (1788-1832), who although junior to Constable by twelve years, had many characteristics in common with him. When Constable, in a letter to Leslie shortly after Fisher's death, described him as 'a good advisor though impetuous, and a truly religious man', he might have been talking about himself. There is no doubt that Fisher respected the straightforwardness and upright self-respect of his friend, and in their extensive correspondence he never himself hesitated to speak his mind. After endless difficulties and delays over Constable's engagement to Maria Bicknell, Fisher decided that he should be galvanized into action. Constable had told Farington on 1st July 1816, that, "under all circumstances he had made up his mind to marry Miss Bicknell witht. further delay and take the chance of what might arise. He said they should have abt. £400 pr. annum." Fisher then wrote to him on 27th August 1816, in these friendly but unequivocal terms, 'get to your lady, and instead of blundering out long sentences about the "Hymenal alter" etc.; say that on Wednesday, September 25th you are ready to marry her. If she replies, like a sensible woman, as I suspect she is, "well, John, here is my hand, I am ready, – all well and good." ' The result was that after a five year engagement, they were married within six weeks of receipt of the letter. Fisher always had the greatest admiration for Constable's work and was full of enthusiastic support at times when the artist's self-confidence might well have been wavering. He had a broader viewpoint and was better educated than Constable, and yet there is never any tone of condecension or forbearance in his attitude.

Constable and Maria Bicknell had made their attachment known in November 1811. At that time the artist had little money apart from the small allowance from his father, and his own almost non-existent earnings. Maria's grandfather, the Rev. Dr. Rhudde, rector of East Bergholt, was a rich old man, who didn't care for the idea of his grand-daughter becoming engaged to an impoverished artist, and the father, Charles Bicknell, who was Solicitor to the Admiralty, living at Spring Gardens, London, appears to have been torn between a wish to accommodate his daughter's feelings, and an even stronger desire not to jeopordize the family expectations by antagonising Dr. Rhudde. Maria's part in all this was one of unimpassioned common sense. She pointed out to Constable that although she admired him, she had a respectful duty towards her parent, and that anyway it was no use their contemplating getting married without enough money. The long engagement soured Constable towards Maria's family, and contributed towards his every ready feeling of injustice. In January 1816 he wrote to her, "I wish you had married me before now, and depend upon it we shall act most unwisely in deferring it much longer—our enemies are busy, vigilant and unprincipled—therefore we know not what we have opposed to us. We cannot be worse off—our peace is already gone and our constitutions fast following—can any money make amends for our loss?" But Maria replied, "Papa says if we remain as we are, he has no idea the Doctor (Rhudde) will alter his will, let us await any time sooner than that you experience the misery of being very much in debt, added to having *a very delicate wife?*" Fisher performed the ceremony at St. Martin-in-the-Fields on the 2nd October 1816, and the couple set off on their honeymoon in the south of England, eventually joining Fisher and his young wife at the Vicarage at Osmington, near Weymouth. In retrospect, this moment seemed to Constable to have been one of the happiest in his life. He spent a lot of time out of doors sketching, or taking walks with Fisher, cf. *Weymouth Bay* (plate 11) and *Rough Sea, Weymouth* (plate 12). John and Maria Constable stayed with the Fishers for six weeks and then returned to London, visiting Bishop Fisher at Salisbury, and calling on John Fisher's father-in-law, the Rev. Dr. Cookson at Binfield in Berkshire.

The couple lived in Constable's bachelor lodgings at 63 Charlotte Street while they were looking for a house, and in 1817 they found No. 1 Keppel Street, off Russell Square, which they were to occupy for the next five years. As the family increased in size, the house became more and more cramped, and Constable said of it, "we wanted room—and were like 'bottled wasps upon a southern wall'—but the five happiest and most interesting years of my life were passed in Keppel Street. I got my children and my fame in that house, neither of which I would exchange with any other man."

With a growing family to support, and sensing that his art was now sufficiently well grounded, he embarked at this period on a group of full size canvases which were intended to ensure his reputation and to reward him financially. The paintings which emerged from his studio during the next decade are among the best known of his works. They were painted from sketches and drawings, many of which had been made in earlier years, during his summer visits to East Bergholt. As a group they illustrate broadly his love of the Stour Valley. The subjects were all taken from canal and river scenes in the vicinity of his birthplace. *The White Horse* (1819), was succeeded by *Stratford Mill* (1820), *The Hay Wain* (1821), *View on the Stour near Dedham* (1822), *The Lock* (1824) and *The Leaping Horse* (1825). When one considers Constable's background, these large works appear as *tours de force* and are remarkable for their nobility. Yet there is in some of them an undeniably popular element; a 'pretty rusticity' which bears evidence of how far he was prepared to go to meet the requirements of the public and of contemporary taste in England. C. R. Leslie, reflecting current opinion, said of his *Waterloo Bridge*, "—it wanted one (quality) which generally constituted the greatest charm of his pictures—*sentiment*—and it was condemned by the public." But Constable invariably regretted any concessions to his artistic integrity, and he is often to be found rebuking himself on the subject in his letters. Late in life he judged himself harshly with the phrase, 'I have too much preferred the picturesque to the beautiful'.

In 1819 Constable was elected Associate of the Royal Academy. He was forty-three at the time of his election and had already presented himself on four occasions, unsuccessfully. He rented a cottage at Hampstead for the first time in the autumn of this year, and despite the financial strain of keeping up two establishments, he continued this practice in the ensuing years to provide open surroundings and fresh air for his wife and children as a palliative to their cramped, unhealthy London quarters, and also to give himself more variety of subject matter to paint. Maria Constable's allowance from her father was replaced by a slightly more substantial income from Dr. Rhudde's will, and Constable had the good fortune to sell *The White Horse*, his first six-foot canvas, which he exhibited at the Royal Academy in 1819. The buyer was Archdeacon Fisher and this characteristic and encouraging gesture from his generous-minded friend was deeply appreciated by the artist.

Largely owing to the activities in his studio, there was a falling off in the production of the open air sketches in the first few years after Constable's marriage, and it was only when he started visiting Hampstead that they resumed their importance in his output. *Hampstead Heath: Morning* (plate 14) was one of Constable's earliest sketches at Hampstead. The commission is documented in a letter in which the modest patrons are named. They were friends of the family in Suffolk; a parson and his wife called Mellinson.

Constable took his family to No. 2 Lower Terrace, Hampstead, in 1821. Sketching on Hampstead Heath, and watching the changing skies, the idea germinated in his mind of undertaking a scientific and methodical study of cloud formations. "I have done a good deal of skying", he told Fisher, and added, "I am determined to conquer all difficulties and that among the rest." He started by making compositions like *Study of Sky and Trees at Hampstead* (plate 15), where the sky is viewed behind trees and rooftops. The following year, he painted a large series of pure cloud studies in oil on paper, cf. *Study of Clouds* (plate 24), and *Study of Cirrus Clouds* (plate 25). On the 7th October 1822 Constable wrote to Fisher, "I have made about fifty carefull studies of *skies*, tolerably large to be carefull." They mostly bear notation stating the time of day, the weather, the direction of the wind, etc. Apart from perfecting Constable's technique in cloud painting, they were intended to serve as studies for the skies in his large canvases. These sketches are an epitaph to

Constable's rationalism, and demonstrate how deeply his romanticism was rooted in the eighteenth century.

In 1822 Constable moved into Farington's old house at 35 Charlotte Street. This was to be his town house for the rest of his life. He resided there with his family during the short winter days. The early part of the year saw him occupied in his studio preparing for the Royal Academy exhibitions, but in the summer months he joined his family whenever he could at Hampstead or later at Brighton, and indulged his pleasure in sketching from nature, an activity which came to him as naturally as breathing. But he was torn between this life of open air activity and family companionship, and the urge to execute large exhibition paintings. He deeply wanted public recognition, and felt that when he was before a six foot canvas, he was really working towards a worthwhile aim.

Constable's reputation in England centred largely around a few devotees and friends, but in 1824 he found a group of enthusiastic admirers in Paris. John Arrowsmith, a picture dealer of English origin living in Paris, was in London early in 1822, and there saw *The Hay Wain*, which Constable had sent to the Royal Academy the year before but which had failed to sell. By 1824 terms had been arrived at whereby Arrowsmith obtained *The Hay Wain, A Lock on the Stour*, and a *Hampstead Heath*, and he took them off at the end of May to be exhibited in Paris. He and another Paris dealer named Schroth were so convinced that Constable's work would cause a stir in the French capital, that they bought a further group of his paintings, probably sketches, to take home with them for stock. Referring to Arrowsmith's purchases, Constable wrote to Fisher on the 17th January 1824, "His object is to make a show of them in Paris—perhaps to my advantage—for a prophet is not known in his own country." Fisher shrewdly replied, "The stupid English public, which has no judgement of its own, will begin to think that there is something in you if the French make your works national property. You have long laid under a mistake. Men do not purchase pictures because they admire them, but because others covet them."

The pictures exhibited at the Salon in Paris were a great success, and Constable was awarded a gold medal by King Charles X. The highest praises came from Géricault and Delacroix, both of whom recognised in Constable's work an original style. Géricault, who saw *The Hay Wain* at the Royal Academy in 1821, "returned quite overwhelmed by one of the great landscapes he went over to see", and Delacroix declared in his *Journal*, after visiting the Salon of 1824, "that man Constable has done me a world of good."

Because of his reception in Paris, Constable has sometimes been considered as the man who inspired the Barbizon painters and the French Impressionists. No matter how much he may have appeared to anticipate them, this view is in danger of missing the point. The stifling influence of the increasingly powerful *bourgoisie* in restoration France brought about its own reaction in certain French artistic circles, and it was among these men that Constable was recognised as a kindred spirit. In a letter to Théophile Silvestre, Delacroix wrote, "He (Constable) and Turner are true reformers. They have got out of the rut of the old landscape paintings. Our school has greatly profited by their example". Constable's open air sketching was not altogether an innovation, for Corot was painting *en plein air* at about the same time. In one respect, however, he foreshadowed the Impressionists in their scientific attempts to break up light into its component parts. As far as is known, Constable never investigated the scientific theory of the reflection of light but, as Delacroix explained in his *Journal,* "He said that the superiority of his fields lay in the fact that they were composed of a multitude of different greens. The failure of the common run of landscape painters to give intensity and life to their greenery results from their making it one uniform colour. What he says about the green of the fields". Delacroix added, "can be applied to the other tones."

Constable first sent his wife and children to Brighton in the summer of 1824. It was hoped that the sea air would prove a tonic for Maria, whose health had lately further declined. She was suffering from sleeplessness and the profuse night sweats characteristic of pulmunary tuberculosis. Constable hated the separation and kept a diary to inform 'Fish' (his pet name for his wife), and his 'chicks' of his everyday activities. Whenever he could find time, he took the coach down to Brighton. Under the patronage of the Prince Regent, the town had become a fashionable seaside resort, and there was a good coach service to and from London. From his correspondence, it is evident that Constable found the place noisy and vulgar, but he was attracted by the soft, clear light, and the sight of the waves breaking on the beach, cf. *Brighton Beach* (plate 27) and *Brighton Beach, with Colliers* (plate 28). His sketches of this period have a peculiar poignancy in that, like the symptoms of his wife's terminal illness, they manifest a last bright flickering of the spirit.

Because Maria was no longer well enough to undertake the journey to Brighton, Constable rented No. 40 Well Walk, Hampstead, in August 1827, keeping it on until the end of his life. The move exerted a strong financial strain, but he said of the house, "It is to my wife's heart's content". Five months later she bore him their seventh and last child. The confinement had further reduced her strength, and the writing was on the wall when he wrote to the printseller and dealer, Dominic Colnaghi, on 15th September 1828, "Her progress towards amendment is sadly slow, but still they tell me that she does mend. Pray God this may be the case – I am much worn by anxiety." When Leslie visited them at Well Walk two months later he says he saw Maria Constable, "on a sofa in their cheerful parlour, and although Constable appeared in his usual spirits in her presence, yet before I left the house, he took me into another room, wrung my hand and burst into tears." A few days later on the 28th November 1828, she died. A profound change overcame Constable after his wife's death. The joy went out of his life and with it faded the spontaneous urge to make sketches from nature.

In Febuary 1829, Constable was elected to full membership of the Academy. It was his fourth attempt and he only scraped home by one vote. As was customary after election, he called upon the President. Lawrence had filled this post since West's death in 1820. He did not share West's warm understanding of Constable's nature, and Constable had to listen to a patronizing lecture to the effect that he must consider himself fortunate, as a painter of the humblest class of landscape, to find preferment over historical painters of great merit. Constable was hurt and insulted, and later wrote to Leslie that he was still 'smarting' under his election. Turner, whom Constable admired but never really liked, called to congratulate him to his face, but wrote about his election in a different vein to Eastlake, one of the unsuccessful candidates.

By the autumn of 1829 Constable had decided, against Fisher's advice, to have a number of paintings engraved in mezzotint. As with Turner's

Liber Studiorum, the motive was to make his reputation safe with posterity. The man selected to do the work was an engraver called David Lucas. He was in fact a happy choice. Lucas worked from a pure mezzotint ground, and through this medium, together with use of drypoint, he acquired rich velvety tones. They blended in a chiaroscuro which admirably illustrated Constable's effects, translated into black and white. The resultant work, entitled *English Landscape,* is little known today. Indeed prints which form the series, and which have considerable charm, have become quite rare. The start of the relationship with Lucas went well enough, and Constable wrote, "His great urbanity and integrity are only equalled by his skill as an engraver; and the scenes now transmitted by his hand are such as I have ever preferred. For the most part, they are those with which I have the strongest associations– those of my earliest years, when 'in the cheerful morn of life, I looked to nature with unceasing joy' ". Unhappily the episode was later marked by a series of meddling, irritable letters from Constable, in which he neurotically accused Lucas of trying to ruin him financially. The charge was particularly unfair, as Constable had inherited a considerable sum indirectly from Dr. Rhudde's fortune, after his wife's death. The fact was that Constable's purpose had changed since he had painted the sketches of his earlier years. He now sought more dramatic effects, and he kept altering proofs, until the unfortunate Lucas was almost at a loss to know what was required of him. Referring to the latest proof of *A Summerland,* cf. (plate 13) which he had been correcting, Constable wrote to Lucas, "I fear I shall be obliged to reject it–it has never recovered from its first trip up–and the sky with the new ground is and ever will be as rotten as cow dung." When Lucas asked for payment for work on rejected plates, Constable launched into bitter accusations. "We all have our foibles and our failings," he told him, "and love of money has always seemed to me to be yours." The set of *English Landscape* prints included *A Summerland* cf. (plate 13), *Autumnal Sunset* cf. (plate 6) and *Weymouth Bay* cf. (plate 11).

The last years of Constable's life were clouded by loneliness and depression. He formed one new friendship. This was with his namesake George Constable, who bought the sombre *Hampstead after a Thunderstorm* (plate 31), and who invited Constable to stay with him at his home

at Arundel in 1834 and 1835. Many of his limited circle of friends were dead. Archdeacon Fisher, who had visited and written to him constantly since 1811, died of cholera in 1832. Much of our knowledge of Constable's day to day thoughts and activities derive from his letters, particularly those to his wife and to Fisher. Leslie's biography fills in the events of the last years, but tactfully understates Constable's increasing irritability and morbidity. His depressions were aggravated by attacks of ill health, particularly rheumatic pain. He performed his function of visitor to the Life Class at the Royal Academy in 1831 and 1837, and lectured at Hampstead, Worcester and to the Royal Institution on the subject of the 'History of Landscape Painting'. It appears from a letter to George Constable dated December 12th 1836, that he was preparing a lecture on clouds and skies which, had he lived, would have been delivered at Hampstead the following summer. In this letter he recommends George Constable to read Forster's *Researches about Atmospheric Phaenomena*. (Forster's classification of clouds was based on Luke Howard's work). John Constable's death occurred suddenly, apparently from violent indigestion, at the age of sixty on the night of the 31st March 1837.

Constable's reputation, which had been mercurial and localised during his life time, slumped completely at his death. At his sale in 1838, many of the pictures were lotted together in undescribed groups, and were bought in for the family at paltry figures. A group of friends and admirers formed a subscription and purchased *The Cornfield* at the artist's sale, presenting it to the then recently formed National Gallery. The public, insofar as they had admired his work, liked it for its rustic associations. Now he was dead, they looked to artists like Creswick, Shayer, Lee and Witherington–'those amiable pot-boiling tradesmen', as Holmes called them, 'who took care to eliminate everything which might conflict with the air of simpering prosperous respectability, which the patriotic Briton expected from the agricultural classes."

Six years after Constable's death, C. R. Leslie published his charming *Memoirs of the Life of John Constable R.A.* The book mostly comprised Constable's correspondence, but the letters were carefully edited to remove any stings, and the whole, with illustrations of his works, made an eminently readable Victorian biography. The book proved popular, and a second unillustrated, but enlarged edition came out two years later, in 1845. If there had been more of Constable's work accessible to public view (forgeries were already on the market in some numbers by 1845), his reputation might have undergone some sort of revaluation, but any hope of this unlikely event was dashed by Ruskin, whose admiration for Turner was so single-minded that it admitted no place for just comparison. He stupidly accused Constable of lacking the very artistic virtues he possessed so strongly. "Unteachableness seems to have been a main feature of his character", he said, "and there is a corresponding want of veneration for Nature herself. His early education and associations were also against him; they induced in him a morbid preference for subjects of a low order."

It was not until 1901, fifty-six years after the appearance of Leslie's biography, and thirteen years after Miss Isabel Constable's bequest to the Victoria and Albert Museum, that a new book on Constable appeared. In this short and sympathetic monograph, Sir Charles Holmes sought, with his characteristic perceptiveness, to trace the origins of Constable's style, and to re-appraise his work in the light of later artistic developments. The following year Holmes pursued the discussion in a much fuller study, entitled *Constable and his Influence on Landscape Painting*, adding a chronological list of the artist's chief pictures and dated sketches. Leslie's *Memoirs of the Life of John Constable R.A.,* was re-published in 1937 edited by the Hon. Andrew Shirley, and again in 1951, edited by Mr. Jonathan Mayne. In recent years Mr. R. B. Beckett has painstakingly gone through the Constable correspondence, and made a typescript, which he has deposited with the Library of the Victoria and Albert Museum. This valuable work is being published by stages. Important among recent publications, and a standard work on the collection at South Kensington, is Mr. Graham Reynolds's *Catalogue of the Constable Collection in the Victoria and Albert Museum,* published in 1960.

In the commentaries on the plates which follow, sketches at the Victoria and Albert Museum from the Isabel Constable Bequest are identified by their acquisition numbers, and those from the collection of Mr. and Mrs. Paul Mellon by their register numbers. The measurements are sight size, and are given in inches and centimeters, height before width.

I would like to thank Mr. Graham Reynolds for allowing the group of sketches at the Victoria and Albert Museum reproduced here to be specially photographed for this book. I am particularly indebted to Mr. Paul Mellon, not only for giving permission to have his sketches photographed and reproduced, but also for his generous encouragement and help over a long period. Among those who have provided me with information and assistance are Sir Colin Anderson, Mr. R. B. Beckett, Mr. Randolph Churchill, Sir Kenneth Clark, Miss L. Harris, Mr. Michael Robinson, Mr. Rae Smith and Miss Dorothy White. I am grateful to my wife for typing the manuscript. Mr. Basil Taylor has kindly read the text, and made suggestions.

Chronology

1776 Born at East Bergholt, June 11th.

1795 (?) First meeting with Sir George Beaumont Bt.

1796 Met J. T. 'Antiquity' Smith while staying with an uncle at Edmonton.

1799 Came to London and was introduced to Joseph Farington, who arranged that he should be admitted as a probationer at the Royal Academy Schools.

1800 Enrolled as a student at the Academy Schools. First visit to Helmingham Park, Suffolk, seat of the Earl of Dysart.

1801 Visited Derbyshire in August.

1802 Exhibited for the first time at the Royal Academy.

1803 Journey from Dover to Deal aboard the East Indiaman *Coutts*.

1804 or 5 Altarpiece for Brantham Church.

1806 Visited the Lake District in September and October.

1807 Copied family portraits by Reynolds, Hoppner and others for Lord Dysart.

1809 Altarpiece for Nayland Church. Visited Malvern Hall, Warwickshire, home of Henry Greswolde Lewis.

1811 At East Bergholt in the summer. Stayed with Bishop Fisher at Salisbury in September and there met the Bishop's nephew, John Fisher. Made his engagement to Maria Bicknell known in November. Took lodgings at 63 Charlotte Street, London in December.

1812-16 Visits to Bergholt.

1815 Death of the artist's mother in March.

1816 Death of the artist's father in May. John Fisher (installed as Archdeacon of Berkshire on the 6th December of this year) married Constable and Maria Bicknell on 2nd October at St. Martin-in-the-Fields, London, and the honeymoon was spent with the Fishers at the Vicarage at Osmington, Dorset.

1817 Moved to 1 Keppel Street, Russell Square, London.

1819 Elected A.R.A. Rented Albion Cottage, Upper Heath, Hampstead in August. Exhibited *The White Horse* at the Royal Academy, (the picture purchased by Archdeacon Fisher).

1820 Visited Archdeacon Fisher at Salisbury in July and August; stayed with Henry Greswolde Lewis and his sister the dowager Countess of Dysart at Malvern Hall, Warwickshire, in September, and joined his family at Hampstead in October. Exhibited *Stratford Mill* at the Royal Academy.

1821 Visited East Bergholt in April. Accompanied Fisher on the Visitation of Berkshire in June, and joined his family at 2 Lower Terrace, Hampstead, from August until October. Visited Fisher again at Salisbury in November. Exhibited *The Hay Wain* at the Royal Academy.

1822 With his family at 2 Lower Terrace, Hampstead, from July until October. Moved his town residence from 1 Keppel Street to Farington's old house, 35 Charlotte Street, London. Exhibited *View on the Stour near Dedham*.

1823 With his family at Stamford Lodge, Hampstead, in June and October. Spent August and September with Fisher at Gillingham, and October and November with Sir George Beaumont at Coleorton Hall, Leicestershire.

1824 Settled his family for the first time at Brighton for the summer and autumn, visiting them intermittantly from May until August. Visited Lady Dysart at Ham House in May. Exhibited *The Haywain, Lock on the Stour*, and *Hampstead Heath* in Paris. Awarded a gold medal by Charles X.

1825 Exhibited *The Leaping Horse* at the Royal Academy. Gained a second gold medal with *The White Horse* at Lille.

1825-8 Visits to Brighton.

1827-37 Rented a small house, 40 Well Walk, Hampstead.

1828 Maria Constable died on 28th November.

1829 Elected Royal Academician in February. Visited Lady Dysart at Ham House in April. Visited the Fishers at Salisbury in July and November. Commenced work with David Lucas on the engraved series *English Landscape*.

1830 Served on the hanging and selection committee of the Royal Academy. The first and second numbers of *English Landscape* published.

1831 Visitor at the Life Class of the Royal Academy. Third and Fourth numbers of *English Landscape* published.

1832 Death of Archdeacon Fisher in August. Fifth number of *English Landscape* published.

1833 Delivered a lecture on the 'Outline of the History of Landscape Painting', at the Hampstead Assembly Rooms in June.

1834 Stayed with his patron and namesake George Constable at Arundel in July, and visited Lady Dysart at Ham House and Lord Egremont at Petworth in September. Exhibited at Worcester.

1835 Visited George Constable at Arundel in July. Exhibited and lectured at Worcester.

1836 Delivered a course of four lectures on the 'History of Landscape Painting' at the Royal Institution, London, in May and June, and gave his second lecture on landscape painting to the Literary and Scientific Institution at Hampstead in July.

1837 Visitor at the Life Class of the Royal Academy. Died suddenly 31st March.

Select Bibliography

General

1845 C. R. LESLIE *Memoirs of the Life of John Constable Esq., R.A., composed chiefly from his Letters*, Longman, Brown, Green & Longmans, London, 2nd ed., (enlarged), 363 pp.

1901 C. J. HOLMES *Constable*, The Sign of the Unicorn, London, 35 pp., 24 pl.

1902 C. J. HOLMES *Constable and his Influence on Landscape Painting*, Constable & Co., London, 252 pp., pl., app.

1903 LORD WINDSOR *John Constable R.A.*, The Walter Scott Publishing Co. Ltd., London, 231 pp., 21 pl.

1921 C. J. HOLMES *Constable, Gainsborough and Lucas*, Whittingham and Griggs, London, 33 pp., 14 pl.

1937 C. R. LESLIE ed. SHIRLEY *Memoirs of the Life of John Constable R.A.*, ed. The Hon. Andrew Shirley, The Medici Society, London, 440 pp., 151 pl.

1948 S. J. KEY *John Constable: his Life and Art*, Pheonix House, London, 127 pp., pl.

1950 K. BADT *John Constable's Clouds*, Routledge & Co., London, 102 pp., 8 pl.

1951 C. R. LESLIE ed. MAYNE *Memoirs of the Life of John Constable R.A.*, ed. Jonathan Mayne, Phaidon Press, London, 434 pp., 72 pl.

1952 R. B. BECKETT *John Constable and the Fishers*, Routledge & Co., London, 300 pp., 8 pl.

1956 R. B. BECKETT Annotated typescript deposited in the library of the Victoria and Albert Museum under the title of the *Correspondence and other Memorials of John Constable R.A.* (The Suffolk Records Society is, by stages, to publish the work in its entirety).
i. Some Early Friends.
ii. Family Letters, 1807-1816.
iii. Maria Bicknell.
iv. Family Correspondence, 1816-1824.
v. Journals to his Wife and Family Correspondence, 1824-1826.
vi. Corrections and Additions to *John Constable and the Fishers*.
vii. C. R. Leslie R.A.
viii. David Lucas.
ix. Family Correspondence, 1826-1837 (with later additions).
x. Some Later Friends.
xi. The Constable Children and Charles Boner.
xii. Patrons.
xiii. Dealers.
xiv. Other Artists.
xv. Constable's Discourses.

1962 R. B. BECKETT *John Constable's Correspondence, the Family at East Bergholt*, H.M.S.O. London, 337 pp., 4 pl.

1964 R. B. BECKETT *John Constable's Correspondence II, Early Friends and Maria Bicknell (Mrs. Constable)*, Suffolk Records Society, Vol. VI, 474 pp., 9 pl.

Catalogues

1904 F. WEDMORE *Constable: Lucas: with a descriptive Catalogue of the Prints they did between them*, P. & D. Colnaghi, London, 59 pp.

1930 A. SHIRLEY *The Published Mezzotints of David Lucas after John Constable R.A.*, Clarendon Press, Oxford, 271 pp., 50 pl.

1960 G. REYNOLDS *Catalogue of the Constable Collection in the Victoria and Albert Museum*, H.M.S.O., London, 260 pp., 310 pl.

Exhibition Catalogues

1934	ROYAL ACADEMY	*Commemorative Catalogue of the Exhibition of British Art.*
1937	TATE GALLERY	*Centenary Exhibition of Paintings and Water-colours by John Constable R.A.*
1937	WILDENSTEIN	*Centenary Memorial Exhibition: John Constable R.A.—his Origins and Influence.*
1938	MUSEE DU LOUVRE	*La Peinture Anglaise XVIIIe & XIXe Siècles.*
1946	ART INSTITUTE OF CHIGAGO	*Masterpieces of English Painting—Hogarth, Constable, Turner.*
1951	ROYAL ACADEMY	*The First Hundred Years of the Royal Academy.*
1956	MANCHESTER CITY ART GALLERY	*John Constable.*
1963	MUSEUM OF FINE ARTS, RICHMOND, VIRGINIA	*Painting in England 1700-1850. The Collection of Mr. and Mrs. Paul Mellon.*
1964-5	ROYAL ACADEMY	*Painting in England 1700-1850.*

General Reference

1905	A. GRAVES	*The Royal Academy Exhibitors, 1769-1904,* Henry Graves & Co., London, Vol. II, pp. 123-5.
1908	A. GRAVES	*Exhibitors at the British Institution for Promoting the Fine Arts in the United Kingdom, 1806-1867,* London, George Bell and Son, pp. 113-4.
1922-28	J. GRIEG	*The Farington Diaries,* Hutchinson & Co., London, 8 Vols. (The published edition as an abbreviation of the MS. in the Royal Collection at Windsor Castle).
1928	W. T. WHITLEY	*Art in England 1800-1820,* Cambridge University Press.
1930	W. T. WHITLEY	*Art in England 1821-1837,* Cambridge University Press.

PLATES

1 East Bergholt Fair, seen from Golding Constable's House

July 1811. Oil on canvas, 6¾ × 14 inches (17·2 × 35·5 cm.), London, Victoria and Albert Museum No. 128–1888 (Isabel Constable Bequest).

A label on the stretcher is inscribed *Painted in 1811;* this is presumably based on an inscription on the back of the original canvas. The canvas has since been relined.

Exhibited: Tate Gallery, *Centenary Exhibition of Paintings and Watercolours by John Constable R.A.,* 1937, No. 132.

Literature: C. J. Holmes, *Constable and his Influence on Landscape Painting,* London, 1902, p. 242, (dated 1811), Pl. opp. p. 27.
Graham Reynolds, *Catalogue of the Constable Collection in the Victoria and Albert Museum,* London, 1960, No. 101, p. 67, Pl. 60.

In the early nineteenth century there used to be a fair each year at East Bergholt. It took place at the end of July for the sale of toys, etc. The large house on the left closely answers the description of Stour House (formerly called West Lodge) East Bergholt, and has been identified as such by the present owner, Mr. Randolph Churchill, and by Miss L. Harris, a resident of East Bergholt, who lived in the house as a child. There is a view of the same house in the collection of Mr. and Mrs. Paul Mellon, which, when it appeared in the H. L. Fison Sale at Christie's (6th Nov. 1959 (13)) was called *Wooling Hall.* But there is no house of this description recorded, and the name may have been a misreading from a defaced label. Another view of the house was in the H. A. C. Gregory Sale at Sotheby's (20th July 1949 (117)) where it was incorrectly described as *Constable's Birth-place, East Bergholt.*

A version of No. 1, but seen at night, is in the collection of Sir Colin Anderson. The top of the tree in the right foreground, which in our version is just a hazy patch, is clearly delineated in the night scene. Both sketches would, therefore, appear to have been painted at an upper window in Golding Constable's house, set back as it was on the north side of the road opposite West Lodge. Constable not infrequently painted from the windows of houses where he was living. Nos. 20 and 21 are views from windows of No. 2 Lower Terrace, Hampstead, and two others, painted from the back of Golding Constable's house, are at Christchurch Mansion Museum, Ipswich.

Three pencil sketches of the fair at East Bergholt are in the Victoria and Albert Museum. Two derive from the sketchbook of 1813 (No. 317–1888 pp. 85 and 87), and one from the sketchbook of the following year (No. 1259–1888 p. 13).

2 Barges on the Stour, with Dedham Church in the Distance

c. 1811. Oil on paper laid on canvas, $10\frac{1}{4} \times 12\frac{1}{4}$ inches ($26 \times 31 \cdot 1$ cm.), London, Victoria and Albert Museum, No. 325–1888 (Isabel Constable Bequest).

Exhibited: Royal Academy, *Exhibition of British Art*, 1934, Cat. No. 379, Pl. CVII.
Tate Gallery, *Centenary Exhibition of Paintings and Watercolours by John Constable R.A.*, 1937, No. 150.

Literature: C. J. Holmes, *Constable and his Influence on Landscape Painting*, London, 1902, p. 242, (dated c. 1810).
C. R. Leslie, *Memoirs of the Life of John Constable R.A.*, ed. Jonathan Mayne, London, 1951, p. 408, Pl. 9.
Graham Reynolds, *Catalogue of the Constable Collection in the Victoria and Albert Museum*, 1960, p. 69, No. 104, Pl. 63.

Reproduced: C. J. Holmes, *Constable*, London, 1901, Pl. XII.
E. V. Lucas, *John Constable the Painter*, London, 1924, Pl. 33.
C. R. Leslie, *Memoirs of the Life of John Constable R.A.*, ed. Andrew Shirley, 1937, Pl. 39.

This atmospheric sketch bears no date. It is placed by Graham Reynolds with *Flatford Mill from a Lock on the Stour*, (Victoria and Albert Museum No. 135–1888) which, from documentary evidence was most likely painted in 1811. In all probability the view represents the lock at Flatford, painted with the artist's back to Flatford Mill. Dating Constable's oil sketches on stylistic grounds is notoriously hazardous, although Holmes's list of 1902, which relied largely on this method, has proved surprisingly accurate in the light of the results of Graham Reynolds's more scientific and factual approach.

The originality of Constable's work has unfortunately been clouded by the accomplishments of later artists, particularly the Barbizon painters and the Impressionists. His contemporaries tended to treat landscape in a conventional manner, and any dramatic content was invariably theatrical in conception. Here, the artist has avoided the obvious device of adding a flash of lightning, and relied instead on subtle lighting effects, and combinations of colours within a limited palette, to achieve the eerie effect of the darkness which comes before a summer rain storm.

3 East Bergholt Church: the Ruined Tower at the West End

(?) c. 1810-15. Oil on canvas, $9\frac{3}{4} \times 13\frac{3}{8}$ inches (24·8 × 34 cm.), London, Victoria and Albert Museum, No. 130–1888 (Isabel Constable Bequest).
The canvas has been relined.

Exhibited: Tate Gallery, *Centenary Exhibition of Paintings and Watercolours by John Constable R.A.*, 1937, No. 139

Literature: C. J. Holmes, *Constable*, London, 1901, p. 17, Pl. XI.
C. J. Holmes, *Constable and his Influence on Landscape Painting*, London, 1902, p. 244, (dated c. 1819).
Graham Reynolds, *Catalogue of the Constable Collection in the Victoria and Albert Museum*, London, 1960, p. 73, No. 112, Pl. 67.

East Bergholt Church, dating from the fourteenth and sixteenth centuries lies only one hundred yards from the site of Golding Constable's house. The church has an unusual feature, in that the bells are housed in a bell cage in the churchyard, and the tower at the west end, where they would normally be placed, is a ruin only rising to about half the height of the nave.

The subject, with its soft coloured brick and stone, was frequently repeated by Constable during his life-time, and a drawing is recorded as early as 1796. Holmes dates this sketch 1819, comparing it with a pencil study in the Victoria and Albert Museum (No. 265–1888). Although the viewpoint is virtually identical, the lack of aerial perspective, which on the left makes the clouds look as if they are on the same plane as the ruined tower, and the muddled handling of the sky on the right, point to an earlier date of production. There is, in fact, a pencil drawing in the Victoria and Albert Museum sketchbook of 1813 (No. 317–1888, p. 24), dated 20th July, in which the poplar trees in the background accord better with those seen in the oil sketch. But as Graham Reynolds points out, No. 3 was probably executed on the spot, and not related to any preliminary drawing.

Constable observed great fidelity to detail, and this scene has hardly changed, apart from the fact that the cottage on the right has gone, and the tree in the churchyard has grown to be taller than the church.

4 Landscape and Double Rainbow

1812. July 28. Oil on paper laid on canvas, $13\frac{1}{4} \times 15\frac{1}{8}$ inches ($33 \cdot 7 \times 38 \cdot 4$ cm.), London, Victoria and Albert Museum, No. 328–1888 (Isabel Constable Bequest).

Inscribed in the top corner in oil by the artist *28 July 1812*. This date is repeated twice on the back: once on the linen backing and once on the stretcher. Also written on the stretcher is *Isey or Min* (Isabel or Minna (Maria), the artist's daughters). The lot number 48/3 is chalked on the back.

Exhibited: Tate Gallery, *Centenary Exhibition of Painting and Watercolours by John Constable R.A.*, 1937, No. 137.

Literature: C. J. Holmes, *Constable and his Influence on Landscape Painting*, London, 1902, p. 242, (dated 1812), Pl. opp. p. 64.
Graham Reynolds, *Catalogue of the Constable Collection in the Victoria and Albert Museum*, London, 1960, p. 75, No. 117, Pl. 69.

Reproduced: C. R. Leslie, *Memoirs of the Life of John Constable R.A.*, ed. Andrew Shirley, London, 1937, Pl. 46.

Referring to his sketches, Constable once said, "I find dirt destroys them a good deal". The paper on which many of the sketches were painted was only secured onto the lid of his painting box by pins at the four corners (the pin-marks can be clearly seen in plate 16). Constable worked to catch rapidly passing effects, and when the sketches had dried and been varnished, they must have been as brittle as dead leaves. He had to lay them down on some more durable material. In this instance he has fixed the torn paper onto a canvas, removed the canvas from its stretcher in order to enlarge the composition, painted out the damages at the upper left and lower right corners and added a windmill. The sketch was later laid down again on linen. The work of preservation was often continued after the artist's death by museum authorities and picture restorers, although an unfortunate result has been that the inscriptions which Constable was in the habit of writing on the back were frequently not transcribed.

Constable was interested in the phenomenon of the rainbow throughout his life. Apart from the present example, No. 10, *A Rainbow—(?) View on the Stour*, and No. 20, *The Grove, or Admiral's House, Hampstead*, there are five drawings at the Victoria and Albert Museum in which rainbows appear, ranging as late as the watercolour *Stonehenge* of 1836, (Victoria and Albert Museum No. 1629–1888).

The mark 48/3, chalked on the back of the canvas indicates that, together with two other items, it formed lot 48 at the executor's sale of the artist's work on 16 May 1838. With the other two, a moonlight scene and a landscape, it was bought in for the family by C. R. Leslie for five guineas.

5 Landscape: the Trees and Cottages under a Lowering Sky

1812, August 6. Oil on canvas laid on millboard, $3\frac{5}{8} \times 9\frac{1}{2}$ inches ($9 \cdot 2 \times 24 \cdot 1$ cm.), London, Victoria and Albert Museum, No. 324–1888 (Isabel Constable Bequest).

Inscribed upper R. by the artist *Augt 6. 1812.*

Exhibited: Tate Gallery, *Centenary Exhibition of Paintings and Watercolours by John Constable R.A.*, 1937, No. 118 (a).

Literature: C. J. Holmes, *Constable and his Influence on Landscape Painting*, London, 1902, p. 241, (dated 1810).
Graham Reynolds, *Catalogue of the Constable Collection in the Victoria and Albert Museum*, London, 1960, p. 76, No. 119, Pl. 71.

Reproduced: C. J. Holmes, *Constable*, London, 1901, Pl. VII.

Constable was at East Bergholt from mid-June until the 22nd August 1812. No. 4, *Landscape and double Rainbow,* and No. 5 are among a group of six dated sketches at the Victoria and Albert Museum painted at this time, and No. 6, *Autumnal Sunset,* although it bears no date, may be included in the group. On 22nd July 1812, the artist wrote to Maria Bicknell, "How much real delight I have had with the study of Landscape this summer. Either I am myself improved in 'the art of seeing Nature' (which Sir Joshua Reynolds calls painting) or Nature has unveiled her beauties to me with a less fastidious hand".

This sketch successfully captures in its small dimensions the feeling of stillness and dry heat which preceeds the first heavy raindrops of a summer storm, and it demonstrates that Constable was by now fully in control of his palette.

In the *Inventory of Art Objects* of 1888 at the Victoria and Albert Museum, the date in the upper right corner was read as 1818, and this figure was repeated in the catalogue of the exhibition at the Tate Gallery. Holmes read the last figure as an *0*, but Graham Reynolds convincingly states that it must be a *2*.

6 Autumnal Sunset

There is a warm glow of light in this sketch, such as is seen for a brief period before the sun goes down. As in No. 27, *Brighton Beach*, Constable has divided his composition into clearly defined planes over an extended painting surface. This device helps to lend variety of atmosphere to the deepening shadows, and the flight of rooks nicely balances the picture. The composition was further extended at the lower border and on the right when the paper was laid down on canvas.

With No. 4, *Landscape and double Rainbow*, and No. 5, *Landscape: the Trees and Cottages under a lowering Sky*, the sketch fits stylistically into the group of dated works painted in July and August 1812. It was later used for the mezzotint *Autumnal Sunset*, engraved by David Lucas, and published in the fifth number of *English Landscape*, in June 1832. Leslie, speaking of the mezzotint, notes that the subject was sketched in Constable's favourite fields near Bergholt, and that Stoke Church tower can be seen on the right, and Langham Church on the left. These features do not appear in the sketch, but were added on the plate.

Constable's correspondence with Lucas, beginning when the former was already over fifty, throws a very different light on the artist's character in later life from that provided by Leslie's biography. He appears as a man neurotically obsessed with a sense of having been wronged, and he was frequently cantankerous. He meddled endlessly with Lucas's progress proofs, and having earlier failed to master the technique himself, continuously harrassed him with outspoken advice and criticism. Concerning the print of *Autumnal Sunset*, he wrote on 2nd June 1832, "The Evng—is spoiled owing to your having fooled with the Rooks—they were the chief feature—which caused me to adopt the subject—nobody knew what they are—but took them for blemishes on the plate."

c. 1812. Oil on paper and canvas, $6\frac{3}{4} \times 13\frac{1}{4}$ inches (17·1 × 33·6 cm.), London, Victoria and Albert Museum, No. 127–1888 (Isabel Constable Bequest).

A label on the stretcher is inscribed *Autumnal Sunset engraved for the English Landscape*. The picture was engraved by David Lucas and published in *English Landscape* in 1832.

Exhibited: Tate Gallery, *Centenary Exhibition of Paintings and Watercolours by John Constable R.A.*, 1937, No. 94.

Literature: C. J. Holmes, *Constable and his Influence on Landscape Painting*, London, 1902, p. 242, (dated 1812).
Andrew Shirley, *The Published Mezzotints of David Lucas after John Constable R.A.*, Oxford, 1930, p. 173, No. 14, Pl. XIV.
C. R. Leslie, *Memoirs of the Life of John Constable R.A.*, ed. Jonathan Mayne, London, 1951, p. 29, note 1 and p. 181.
Graham Reynolds, *Catalogue of the Constable Collection in the Victoria and Albert Museum*, London, 1960, p. 76, No. 120, Pl. 71.

Reproduced: E. V. Lucas, *John Constable the Painter*, London, 1924, p. 26.

7 Cornfield under heavy Cloud

c. 1813. Oil on canvas, $15\frac{1}{4} \times 22\frac{1}{4}$ inches ($38\cdot7 \times 56\cdot5$ cm.), Upperville, Virginia, Mr. and Mrs. Paul Mellon, No. 62/4/26/4.

Collection: Colonel J. F. Allhusen.

Exhibited: Museum of Fine Arts, Richmond, Virginia, *Painting in England 1700-1850*, 1963, No. 94, Pl. 33.
Royal Academy, London, *Painting in England 1700-1850*, 1964-5, No. 66, Pl. 14.

A light glitter of water can be seen on the horizon of No. 7, and the scene may well have been painted in the neighbourhood of Colchester near the estuary of the river Stour. It is clear from drawings in the sketchbook of 1813 in the Victoria and Albert Museum (No. 317—1888), that Constable made excursions during his residence at East Bergholt this year to Chelmsford, Colchester and Mistley. As Basil Taylor points out, Constable was in the habit of using his sketchbook notes for pictures painted much later in his life, but No. 7 has no direct connexion with any of the drawings in the 1813 sketchbook. As in the case of No. 3, *East Bergholt Church: the ruined Tower at the west end*, it was very likely painted on the spot.

There is a feature in the picture which would suggest the date c. 1813. Constable evidently found difficulty at this time in composing his foregrounds. The rather artificial device of using the corn as a *repoussoir* is repeated on pp. 21, 34, and 64 of the 1813 sketchbook, and in No. 1, *East Bergholt Fair, seen from Golding Constable's House,* where the scene is composed behind a wooden fence.

The towering storm clouds and effective aerial perspective foreshadow the cloud studies of 1821 and 1822.

8 Study of a Cart and Horses, with a Carter and Dog

1814, October. Oil on paper with a brown ground, $6\frac{1}{2} \times 9\frac{3}{8}$ inches (16.5×23.8 cm.), London, Victoria and Albert Museum, No. 332–1888. (Isabel Constable Bequest).

Inscribed on the back in ink with the monogram *JC*.

Exhibited: Tate Gallery, *Centenary Exhibition of Paintings and Watercolours by John Constable R.A.*, 1937, No. 112 (a).

Literature: C. J. Holmes, *Constable and his Influence on Landscape Painting*, London, 1902, p. 242, (dated 1814).
R. B. Beckett, *Burlington Magazine*, Vol. XCVIII, 1956, p. 18.
Graham Reynolds, *Burlington Magazine*, Vol. XCVIII, 1956, p. 132.
Graham Reynolds, *Catalogue of the Constable Collection in the Victoria and Albert Museum*, London, 1960, p. 102, No. 135, Pl. 99.

This sketch is one of a number of studies both in pencil and oils for the *Stour Valley and Dedham Village* in the Museum of Fine Arts, Boston. The Boston picture represents a broad view over the Stour Valley, seen from an elevated position on a road. In the foreground men are shovelling gravel and two horses are harnessed to a cart beside which a dog is seated. As Beckett points out, the scene most likely represents a view of Dedham from the vicinity of Old Hall, East Bergholt.

Beckett has proved that a man named Thomas Fitzhugh commissioned the picture from Constable as a wedding present for his fiancée, Philadelphia, daughter of Peter Godfrey of Old Hall. Constable wrote to Maria Bicknell on 25th October, 1814, "I have almost done a picture of 'the Valley' for Mr. Fitzhugh, (a present for Miss G. to contemplate in London), which I think you would like could you see it".

The artist appears to have taken great pains with the picture, and there are at least eleven studies connected with it. From the evidence of inscriptions, these studies were executed between 5th September and the 9th October, 1814. The Victoria and Albert Museum sketchbook of 1814 (No. 1259–1888) contains drawings of the men digging on pp. 36, 54 and 60; of horses and carts on pp. 54, 68, 73 and 74, and general views of the composition on pp. 62 and 81. Apart from No. 8, there is another oil sketch in the Victoria and Albert Museum (No. 333–1888), dated 24th October 1814, of the cart and horses, but without the man and the dog, and a third, size $15\frac{1}{2} \times 22$ inches, *Vale of Dedham from East Bergholt*, at Temple Newsam House, Leeds, showing the whole scene from a viewpoint slightly to the left of that of the Boston picture.

Constable took immense trouble in trying to preserve accuracy to nature in his finished works. He frequently adopted details from his sketchbooks and used them literally in the preparatory oil studies painted in his studio, and in his finished canvases. This practice occasionally resulted in the transferred details looking rather wooden and out of context in the finished work, as for instance with the ploughman in No. 13, *Dedham Vale with Ploughman*.

A number of Constable's oil sketches were, in fact, made for, or adopted as, studies for larger works, but an attempt has been made to confine the present selection as much as possible to sketches from nature, made as an end in themselves.

9 Study of Flowers in a Glass Vase

(?) c. 1814. Oil on millboard, laid on panel, $19\frac{7}{8} \times 13$ inches ($50\cdot5 \times 33$ cm.), London, Victoria and Albert Museum, No. 581–1888, (Isabel Constable Bequest).

On the back of the panel is a label inscribed *South Kensington Museum Flowers painted by John Constable R.A.*

Literature: C. J. Holmes, *Constable and his Influence on Landscape Painting*, London, 1902, p. 243, (dated c. 1814).
C. R. Leslie, *Memoirs of the Life of John Constable R.A.*, p. 405, Pl. XI.
Graham Reynolds, *Catalogue of the Constable Collection in the Victoria and Albert Museum*, London, 1960, p. 92, No. 130, Pl. 98.

Constable made a number of flower studies. It is impossible to date most of them with any certainty. Apart from the present sketch, there are two others in the Victoria and Albert Museum of wild flowers, (Nos. 582–1888 and 331–1888), as well as a large study of poppies, (No. 329–1888), and two sketches of hollyhocks and tulips are in the collection of Mr. and Mrs. Mellon.

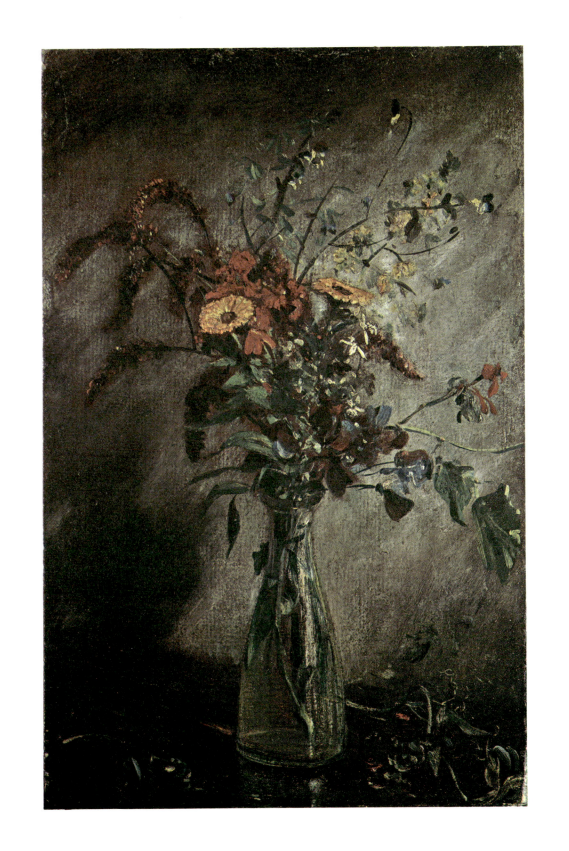

10 A Rainbow–(?) View on the Stour

(?) c. 1813-14. Oil on canvas, 12¾ × 21½ inches (32·5 × 54·5 cm.), Upperville, Virginia, Mr. and Mrs. Paul Mellon, No. 62/3/15/14.

Collections: Eustace Constable.
               W. Cuthbertson.
               Charles Russell.
Exhibited: Museum of Fine Arts, Richmond, Virginia, *Painting in England 1700-1850*, 1963, No. 96, Pl. 44.
               Royal Academy, London, *Painting in England 1700-1850*, 1964-5, No. 70.

There is no documentary evidence accompanying this sketch to give any idea at what date or where it was painted. The statement written on a label on the back, that the tower belonged to East Bergholt church is patently false. The sketch is not altogether different in style from No. 7, *Cornfield under heavy Cloud*, and may have been executed as early as 1813, at the time when Constable was staying at East Bergholt, and when he made his expeditions to Chelmsford, Colchester and Mistley. He was painting again at East Bergholt in 1814.

The sketches painted on canvas were most likely started on the spot and completed in the studio, and this would account for their greater degree of finish.

11 Weymouth Bay

(?) c. 1816. Oil on millboard, $8 \times 9\frac{3}{4}$ inches ($20 \cdot 3 \times 24 \cdot 7$ cm.), London, Victoria and Albert Museum, No. 330–1888 (Isabel Constable Bequest).

Inscribed on the back *JC*.

Subject engraved by David Lucas and published in *English Landscape* in 1830.

Exhibited: Tate Gallery, *Centenary Exhibition of Paintings and Watercolours by John Constable R.A.*, 1937, No. 116 (b).

Literature: C. J. Holmes, *Constable*, 1901, p. 17.
C. J. Holmes, *Constable and his Influence on Landscape Painting*, London, 1902, p. 244, (dated ? 1819).
C. J. Holmes, *Burlington Magazine*, Vol. XVII, 1910, p. 85.
Andrew Shirley, *The Published Mezzotints of David Lucas after John Constable R.A.*, Oxford, 1930, p. 172, No. 13.
C. R. Leslie, *Memoirs of the Life of John Constable R.A.*, ed. Jonathan Mayne, London, 1951, p. 409, Pl. 13.
R. B. Beckett, *Connoiseur*, Vol. CXXIX, 1952, pp. 6-8.
Graham Reynolds, *Catalogue of the Constable Collection in the Victoria and Albert Museum*, London, 1960, p. 111, No. 155, Pl. 127.

The loose handling of the brush and the wild sky would suggest that this is a late sketch. It would further appear to have been made as a study for Lucas's mezzotint, which was published in the first number of *English Landscape* in June 1830. The mezzotint accords well with the dimensions and with the spirit of the sketch. Yet this hypothesis is virtually insupportable on the grounds that a later edition of Lucas's mezzotints, published by Bohn in 1855, states that the original painting from which *Weymouth Bay* was taken, was in the Edwin Bullock Collection. This picture, a full size canvas, passed into the collection at The Louvre. The Louvre version of *Weymouth Bay*, which is close, except in some details to the mezzotint, was rejected as being authentic by P. M. Turner and doubted by Shirley, but is accepted by Graham Reynolds, and it would seem certain that it was in fact used for the print.

Constable exhibited *Osmington Shore, near Weymouth*, a 40×48 inch picture at the British Institution (No. 44), in 1819. Despite its similarity in size to the Louvre picture, it is improbable that they are one and the same. Although Osmington Shore is next to Weymouth Bay, they are separated at Redcliff Point, and such a miss-titling was unlikely to occur in a contemporary exhibition.

There remains a third version of *Weymouth Bay* at the National Gallery (No. 2652). This $21 \times 29\frac{1}{2}$ inch canvas was painted from almost the same view point as No. 11, but is entirely different in character. There are no figures in the foreground and no birds. The land and rock formations are closely observed and the picture has an air of having been painted on the spot. The aerial perspective has almost entirely failed and the shaggy clouds look like a stage backdrop.

A curious feature of the subject is that a shepherd and his flock, easily distinguishable in the National Gallery and the Louvre versions, and in the mezzotint, are represented only as a blob and a streak of white on the far side of the beach in No. 11. It may be that Constable made this sketch as an adaptation from the National Gallery version and as a study for the picture now at the Louvre, and that the Louvre version was later used for the mezzotint.

12 Rough Sea, Weymouth

(?) 1816. Oil on canvas, $8\frac{7}{8} \times 21\frac{7}{8}$ inches 22–5 × 55·5 cm.), Upperville, Virginia, Mr. and Mrs. Paul Mellon, No. 63/5/29/12.
An old label on the back is inscribed *Weymouth Bay*.

Collections: Lionel B. Constable.
             Carlos Peacock.
Exhibited: Museum of Fine Arts, Richmond, Virginia, *Painting in England 1700-1850*, 1963, No. 95, Pl. 40.
             Royal Academy, London, *Painting in England 1700-1850*, 1964-1965, No. 64.
Literature: C. R. Leslie, *Memoirs of the Life of John Constable R.A.*, ed. Jonathan Mayne, London 1951, p. 222.
             R. B. Beckett, *John Constable and the Fishers*, London, 1952, p. 34.

Constable and his wife spent their honeymoon with Constable's friend John Fisher and his wife at Osmington, near Weymouth. The two men were known to have taken long walks together, and it might have been on one of these that they went to the Bill of Portland, some five miles away, and that Fisher related the story of the loss of the East Indiaman *The Earl of Abergavenny*. This ship, according to a contemporary report, was "driven furiously on the rocks off the Bill of Portland", on the 5th February 1805, and lost with three hundred persons and £200,000 worth of cargo. The captain, John Wordsworth, who drowned in the disaster, was brother to the poet and a cousin of John Fisher's wife Mary. There is a tradition that the piece of wreckage on the left of the picture is a reference to this event. The incident was still on the artist's mind when, in 1833, he wrote to Mrs. Leslie, wife of his biographer, enclosing a small gift. "I shall now." he says, "to give value to the fragment I send you, apply to it a line of Wordsworth: 'This sea in anger, and that dismal shore.' I think of Wordsworth, for on that spot perished his brother in the wreck of the *Abergavenny*."

The attribution of No. 12 is accepted here, not on the basis of the associative story alone, but because of the family provenance and the old label on the back stating the location to be Weymouth Bay. This beautiful sketch is obviously too fine in quality to have been painted by another member of the Constable family. It is, however, in some ways uncharacteristic of the artist's work, and serves to stress the difficulties in arriving at attributions on stylistic grounds alone.

13 Dedham Vale with Ploughmen

(?) c. 1817-1825 (based on a painting of 1813-14). Oil on canvas, $16\frac{3}{4} \times 30$ inches (42·5 × 76·2 cm.), Upperville, Virginia, Mr. and Mrs. Paul Mellon, No. 62/3/10/15.

Engraved by David Lucas and published in *English Landscape* in 1831.

Collections: John Allnut.
L. Nevill Long.

Exhibited: Museum of Fine Arts, Richmond, Virginia, *Painting in England 1700-1850*, 1963, No. 92, Pl. 56.
Royal Academy, London, *Painting in England 1700-1850*, 1964-5, No. 59.

Literature: C. J. Holmes, *Constable and his Influence on Landscape Painting*, London, 1902, p. 242, (first version dated 1814).
Andrew Shirley, *The Published Mezzotints of David Lucas after John Constable R.A.*, Oxford, 1930, p. 169, No. 10, Pl. X.
C. R. Leslie, *Memoirs of the Life of John Constable R.A.*, ed. Jonathan Mayne, London, 1951, pp. 47 and 48.
R. B. Beckett, *John Constable's Correspondence, the Family at East Bergholt 1807-1837*, London, 1962, p. 101.

It seems likely that this painting is the reduced replica of the composition exhibited as No. 28 at the Royal Academy in 1814, and called *Landscape— Ploughing Scene in Suffolk*; further that John Allnutt took it in exchange for the original version, which he had bought at the Royal Academy. Confusion has arisen over this subject largely because Allnutt, writing to Leslie twenty-nine years after the Royal Academy exhibition of 1814, recollected that he had bought the first version at the British Institution. Constable had only one landscape at the British Institution in that year, and it was sold to James Carpenter.

On the 22nd February 1814, shortly before the Royal Academy exhibition, Constable wrote to John Dunthorne Snr., "I have added some ploughmen to the landscape from the park pales which is a great help, but I must try and warm the picture a little more if I can. But it will be difficult as 'tis now all of a piece—it is bleak and looks as if there would be a shower of sleet, and that you know is too much the case with my things".

Allnut seems to have shared the artist's discomfort about the sky, and

44

he tells Leslie in his letter of 2nd February 1843, "As I did not quite like the effect of the sky, I was foolish enough to have that obliterated, and a new one put in by another artist, which, though extremely beautiful, did not harmonise with the other parts of the picture. Some years later I got a friend of Mr. Constable to ask him if he would be kind enough to restore the picture to its original state, to which he readily assented. Having a very beautiful painting by Mr. (now Sir Augustus) Callcott, which was nearly the same size, but not quite so high, I sent it to Mr. Constable together with his own, and expressed a wish that, if he could do it without injury to the picture, he would reduce the size of it in height, by lowering the sky, so as to make it nearer the size of Mr. Callcott's, to which I wished it to hang as a companion". He goes on to describe Constable's diffidence about accepting payment and adds that, "wishing to make the picture as acceptable to me as possible, he had, instead of reducing the height of the old picture, painted an entirely new one of the same subject, exactly the size of the one by Callcott; and that if I was satisfied with the exchange, (which of course I was), it gave him much pleasure". The Callcott landscape and No. 13 appeared as lots 474 and 475 respectively in the Allnutt sale at Christie's on the 20th June 1863. The Constable was described as *A Landscape, with a mass of wood in the centre, meadows beyond, and a man ploughing in the foreground; admirable effect of a passing shower—the companion*, (i.e. to lot 474).

The original presumably remained in the artist's studio, and was among the landscapes, many of which were lotted together in un-described groups, at the sale of his work in 1838. A letter from Lucas to George Simms, dated September 1846, indicates that the picture from which Lucas made the mezzotint called *A Summerland* was in the latter's possession by that time. This was probably the earlier version exhibited at the Royal Academy, and it would certainly help to account for the differences between No. 13 and the print in the proportions of height to width and in the treatment of the sky, although the prints frequently did not follow the sketches in either of these points.

The sketchbook of 1813 in the Victoria and Albert Museum (No. 317– 1888) contains a drawing on page 12 of the view of Dedham Vale inscribed *25 July—noon—Suffolk*, and pages 52, 71 and 72 have studies for the ploughmen.

14 Hampstead Heath: Morning

Referring to this sketch the artist wrote on the 1st May 1819, "Some Suffolk friends have just called, Revd. Mellinson and his wife—a nice lady. They have bespoke a small landscape, price 20G's, all a help". In the same month he told his wife in another letter, "Everything seems full of blossom of some kind and at every step I take, and on whatever object I turn my eyes, that sublime expression of the scriptures 'I am the resurrection and the life' seems as it uttered near me."

Constable first started visiting Hampstead in the summer of 1819, and he rented Albion Cottage, Upper Heath, towards the end of August. No. 14 was most likely painted at this time. There was to be a long and close association with Hampstead, and the uneven ground of Hampstead Heath afforded Constable excellent viewpoints for those sketches where the sky played an important part in the composition. Some of the ponds, which derived from local springs, were affected by the activities of the Water Board towards the end of the nineteenth century, and as a result have since dried up. Most of Constable's pond scenes appear to have been painted near Branch Hill Pond on the west side of the Heath, but No. 14 does not answer the description of this spot.

1819. Oil on canvas, $9\frac{1}{2} \times 12\frac{3}{4}$ inches (24 × 32·2 cm.), Upperville, Virginia, Mr. and Mrs. Paul Mellon, No. 62/4/5/17.

Collection: The Reverend P. Mellinson.
Exhibited: Museum of Fine Arts, Richmond, Virginia, *Painting in England 1700-1850*, 1963, No. 100.
Literature: C. R. Leslie, *Memoirs of the Life of John Constable R.A.*, ed. Andrew Shirley, p. 105.

15 Study of Sky and Trees at Hampstead

1821. October 2. Oil on paper, $9\frac{5}{8} \times 11\frac{3}{4}$ inches ($24\cdot5 \times 29\cdot8$ cm.), London, Victoria and Albert Museum, No. 168–1888 (Isabel Constable Bequest).

Inscribed on the back in ink by the artist *Ocr. 2d. 1821. 8. to 9. very fine still morning. turned out a may day. Rode with Revd. Dr. White. round by Highgate, Muswell Hill, Coney Hatch, Finchley. by Hendon Home.* Also inscribed in ink with the monogram *JC*.

Exhibited: Tate Gallery, *Centenary Exhibition of Paintings and Watercolours by John Constable R.A.,* 1937, No. 114 (b).

Literature: C. J. Holmes, *Constable and his Influence on Landscape Painting,* London, 1902, p. 245, (dated 1821).

   Graham Reynolds, *Catalogue of the Constable Collection in the Victoria and Albert Museum,* London, 1960, p. 139, No. 226, Pl. 170.

There is a group of sketches painted in 1821 which preceeds the pure cloud studies of the following year, but in which the sky, behind dense foliage, forms the dominant theme. In this sketch the alto-cumulus formation of clouds is delicately indicated above the still, crisp leaves of the bushes and trees.

Constable had been giving a lot of thought to his skies, and he wrote to Fisher three weeks after painting this sketch saying, "I have done a good deal of skying. I am determined to conquer all difficulties and that among the rest". He realised the importance of his skies, both as a source of light and as a compositional feature, and he goes on in the same letter, "Certainly if the sky is obtrusive, as mine are, it is bad; but if it is evaded, as mine are not, it is worse; it must and always shall with me make an effectual part of the composition. It will be difficult to name a class of landscape in which the sky is not the key note, the standard of scale, and the chief organ of sentiment."

The inscription '8 to 9' on the back of the sketch would appear to imply that it was completed in an hour before Constable set off with a friend on a seven mile ride around the villages of north London.

16 (?) 'The Salt Box', Hampstead

1821, October 13. Oil on paper, $9\frac{3}{4} \times 11\frac{3}{4}$ inches (24·8 × 28·8 cm.), London, Victoria and Albert Museum, No. 781–1888 (Isabel Constable Bequest).

Inscribed on the back in pencil by the artist, *Octr – 13th. 1821.– 4 to 5 afternoon – very fine with Gentle Wind at N.E.* The inscription is repeated in ink in another hand.

Exhibited: Tate Gallery, *Centenary Exhibition of Paintings and Watercolours by John Constable R.A.*, 1937, No. 122 (b).

Literature: C. J. Holmes, *Constable and his Influence on Landscape Painting*, London, 1902, p. 245, (dated 1821).
Graham Reynolds, *Catalogue of the Constable Collection in the Victoria and Albert Museum*, London, 1960, p. 139, No. 227, Pl. 171.

The scene has tentatively been identified by Graham Reynolds as Hampstead Heath looking towards Harrow, with a view of the house called 'The Salt Box'. The direction of the smoke from the chimney, and the artist's observation that the wind was 'at N.E.', confirm that the view is towards the north-west, and the projection abreast the rise of ground on the horizon at the extreme left would appear to be the spire of Harrow Church. It was not characteristic of Constable to deviate from accurate topographical representation in his rapid sketches on paper and the relationship between the house, the pond, and the dividing paths bears a close resemblance to those features in the National Gallery painting (No. 1236), entitled *Hampstead Heath: the House called the 'Salt Box' in the distance*.

Writing of the National Gallery picture, C. R. Leslie exclaims "I have before noticed that what are commonly called warm colours are not necessary to produce the impression of warmth in landscape; and this picture affords, to me, the strongest possible proof of the truth of this. The sky is of the blue of an English Summer day – the distance is of a deep blue, and the nearest trees and grass of the freshest green; for Constable could never consent to parch up the verdure of nature to obtain warmth." The same is true of the Victoria and Albert Museum sketch, yet the technique whereby this effect is arrived at is clearer, and the pink under-painting permeates the sketch with a feeling of the soft heat of an autumnal afternoon.

17 Evening Landscape after Rain

(?) 1821. Oil on paper laid on panel, 7 × 9½ inches (17·7 × 24 cm.), Upperville, Virginia, Mr. and Mrs. Paul Mellon, No. 62/4/19/6.

Collections: Hugh Constable.
                    Mrs. Audrey Weber.

Exhibited: Museum of Fine Arts, Richmond, Virginia, *Painting in England 1700-1850*, 1963, No. 108, Pl. 69.
                    Royal Academy, London, *Painting in England, 1700-1850*, 1964-5, No. 75.

This masterly sketch, a study of golden light under indigo clouds, is here dated (?) 1821 on the grounds that it can be numbered among the sky studies of that period. The flat landscape points against Hampstead as the location. It may, however, have been painted in the neighbourhood of Salisbury, for Constable had joined Fisher there by 15th November 1821, and stayed for a few days before returning to London.

There is an absolute understanding of the aerial perspective, and the volume of the curtain of clouds in the foreground is perfectly suggested. The vague shapes in the landscape melt into the half-light of a late autumn afternoon, and provide an entirely satisfactory low horizon for the dramatic sky.

18 Branch Hill Pond: Evening

c. 1821-2. Oil on paper, $9 \times 7\frac{1}{2}$ inches ($22 \cdot 9 \times 19$ cm.), London, Victoria and Albert Museum, No. 339–1888 (Isabel Constable Bequest).

verso: A Cloud Study.

Exhibited: Tate Gallery, *Centenary Exhibition of Paintings and Watercolours by John Constable R.A.*, 1937, No. 131 (b).

Literature: C. J. Holmes, *Constable and his Influence on Landscape Painting*, London, 1902, p. 248, (dated 1827).
C. R. Leslie, *Memoirs of the Life of John Constable R.A.*, ed. Jonathan Mayne, London, 1951, p. 413, Pl. 31.
Graham Reynolds, *Catalogue of the Constable Collection in the Victoria and Albert Museum*, London, 1960, p. 149, No. 251, Pl. 190.

Reproduced: E. V. Lucas, *John Constable the Painter*, London, 1924, Pl. 41.

54

This view of Branch Hill Pond is taken looking west from Jack Straw's Castle into the setting sun. The predominant tree, which appears in the centre of the composition in No. 19, *Branch Hill Pond, Hampstead*, is seen here on the right of the pond. The pure cloud study on the back of this sketch would indicate that it was not painted later than 1822, when Constable was engaged on his sky studies, and the freeness of handling identifies it with dated work of that period.

Constable repeated the subject of Branch Hill Pond many times during his life (Graham Reynolds mentions six versions in his catalogue, pp. 118-9), and considerable artistic licence appears to have been used in some of them. There are changes in the topography, lighting effects, and in the additions of a windmill and a house.

The earliest version of the subject, which is in the Victoria and Albert Museum (No. 122–1888), dates from October 1819; the period when Constable first went to Hampstead. That sketch and No. 18 were evidently made from nature, but the later canvas of 1828 at the Victoria and Albert Museum (No. F.A.35), although based on No. 122–1888, appears to have freely incorporated the house called 'The Salt Box' which appears in No. 16, *(?) 'The Salt Box', Hampstead*, and which would have been out of view to the right, as is made clear in the present sketch.

Both No. 18 and No. 19, *Branch Hill Pond, Hampstead*, betray the influence of Rubens. Constable had seen Ruben's *Château de Steen* in Sir George Beaumont's collection at Coleorton Hall as early as 1804.

19 Branch Hill Pond, Hampstead

c. 1821-2. Oil on canvas, $9\frac{5}{8} \times 15\frac{1}{2}$ inches (24·5 × 39·4 cm.), London, Victoria and Albert Museum, No. 125–1888 (Isabel Constable Bequest).
The canvas has been relined.
Exhibited: Tate Gallery, *Centenary Exhibition of Paintings and Watercolours by John Constable R.A.*, 1937, No. 106.
Literature: C. J. Holmes, *Constable and his Influence on Landscape Painting*, London, 1902, p. 248, (dated c. 1827).
Graham Reynolds, *Catalogue of the Constable Collection in the Victoria and Albert Museum*, London, 1960, p. 141, No. 233, Pl. 177.

A photograph, which appeared in *The Sketch* of the 20th July 1890, was taken from the same viewpoint as No. 19. It showed a view looking north-west towards Harrow from the flag-staff adjacent to Jack Straw's Castle, and the pond, which has since dried up, in the foreground. The present sketch was probably made about one hundred yards south of No. 16 *(?)* '*The Salt Box*', *Hampstead*. In both views the river Brent can be discerned in the middle distance on the right.

There are several sketches from near identical viewpoints, identifiable on account of the prominent tree in the centre. *Hampstead Heath looking towards Harrow* at the Manchester City Art Gallery is dated August 1821, while another sketch, *Hampstead Heath at Sunset, looking towards Harrow*, undated and taken a little to the left, is in the collection of Mr. and Mrs. Paul Mellon. Two further sketches at the Victoria and Albert Museum, a *View at Hampstead: Evening* (No. 337–1888) and *Hampstead: Stormy sunset* (No. 336–1888) are both dated 31st July 1822.

Holmes dates this sketch c. 1827, but it would appear more likely that it was painted in the late summer of 1821 or 1822, while Constable was at No. 2 Lower Terrace, Hampstead. As in No. 4 *Landscape and double Rainbow*, Constable has extended the surface of the composition by removing the canvas from its original stretcher and painting on the turn-over on either side and at the bottom.

20 The Grove, or Admiral's House, Hampstead

(?) 1821-2. Oil on paper, laid on canvas, $9\frac{5}{8} \times 11\frac{1}{2}$ inches ($24\cdot5 \times 29\cdot2$ cm.), London, Victoria and Albert Museum. No. 137–1888 (Isabel Constable Bequest).

Exhibited: Tate Gallery, *Centenary Exhibition of Paintings and Watercolours by John Constable R.A.*, 1937, No. 140.
Paris, Palais du Louvre, *La Peinture Anglaise XVIIIᵉ et XIXᵉ Siècles*, 1938, No. 31.

Literature: C. J. Holmes, *Constable*, London, 1901, p. 19, Pl. XVIII.
C. J. Holmes, *Constable and his Influence on Landscape Painting*, London, 1902, p. 250, (no date ascribed).
Graham Reynolds, *Catalogue of the Constable Collection in the the Victoria and Albert Museum*, London, 1960, p. 231, No. 402, Pl. 302.

Constable settled his family during the summer of 1821 and 1822 at No. 2 Lower Terrace, Hampstead. This sketch would appear to have been taken from an upper window in the front of the house, as the view of Admiral's House, situated opposite, is obstructed from ground level by a brick wall, which encloses the garden on the north side and which was almost certainly there in Constable's day. The composition of a more finished version, in the Nationalgalerie, Berlin, is extended downwards, as if the artist were conscious that his sketch, taken from an elevated position, lacked foreground.

The house was known as 'The Grove' until about 1911, when the main part was retitled 'Admiral's House', and the lower building in front of it was called 'Grove Lodge'. The cottage on the right with the sloping roof has since gone.

Another view of the house, from a different angle, is in the National Gallery, London, (No. 1246), and Martin Davies suggests that it was probably this picture which Constable exhibited at the Royal Academy in 1832 with the title, 'A romantic house at Hampstead'. On the basis of the exhibited picture, Graham Reynolds dates No. 20 between c. 1830 and 1836.

21 View in a Garden, with a Red House Beyond

(?) 1821-2. Oil on canvas, 14×12 inches (35·5×30·5 cm.), London, Victoria and Albert Museum, No. 136–1888 (Isabel Constable Bequest).
The canvas has been relined.

Exhibited: Tate Gallery, *Centenary Exhibition of Paintings and Watercolours by John Constable R.A.*, 1937, No. 93.
Paris, Palais du Louvre, *La Peinture Anglaise XVIIIᵉ et XIXᵉ Siècles*, 1938, No. 32.

Literature: C. J. Holmes, *Constable*, London, 1901, p. 19, Pl. XVIII.
C. J. Holmes, *Constable and his Influence on Landscape Painting*, London, 1902, p. 244, (dated ? 1817).
Graham Reynolds, *Catalogue of the Constable Collection in the Victoria and Albert Museum*, London, 1960, p. 140, No. 232, Pl. 176.

This is another view from an upper window, and it would seem to have been painted from the back of No. 2 Lower Terrace, looking towards the houses in Upper Terrace, Hampstead. The style of the foliage is closely identifiable with that of No. 15, *Study of Sky and Trees at Hampstead,* which is dated October 2, 1821.

Constable had gone to Hampstead from Keppel Street on 3rd August 1821 and he wrote to Fisher on the following day, "I am as much here as possible with my dear family. My placid and contented companion with her three infants are well". An attractive domestic note is the family washing hanging out under an impending thunderstorm.

The purpose of spending this time at Hampstead was probably partly for the health of his wife and small children, and partly to execute the sky studies for which Hampstead Heath provided a natural observatory. But Constable was restless all the time to get back to his large pictures, on which he hoped to base fame and fortune. He wrote to Fisher in October 1821, "I have not been idle and have made more particular and general study than I have ever done in one summer. But I am most anxious to get into my London painting room", (he had rented a large room in a glazier's shop), "for I do not consider myself at work without I am before a six foot canvas".

22 View in a Garden, with a Shed on the Left

(?) 1821-2. Oil on paper laid on canvas, $11\frac{7}{8} \times 9\frac{3}{8}$ inches (30·2 × 23·8 cm.), London, Victoria and Albert Museum, No. 133–1888 (Isabel Constable Bequest).

The stretcher is inscribed in ink. *On paper. J. Constable R.A. Peel Feb 18 48.5.*

Exhibited: Tate Gallery, *Centenary Exhibition of Paintings and Watercolours by John Constable R.A.*, 1937, No. 153.

Literature: C. J. Holmes, *Constable and his Influence on Landscape Painting*, London, 1902, p. 251 (c. 1834).

              Graham Reynolds, *Catalogue of the Constable Collection in the Victoria and Albert Museum*, London, 1960, p. 140, No. 231, Pl. 175.

Despite the use of the palette knife, which led Holmes to date this sketch c. 1834, the natural colouring and the absence of mannerism in the brush strokes suggest an earlier date. Graham Reynolds places it c. 1821 ?, with the studies of sky and trees executed about that time.

If this sketch and No. 21, *View of a Garden with a red House beyond* were in fact painted at No. 2 Lower Terrace, it would seem that the latter was painted from the window above the shed. Added weight is given to the suggested location by an extract from a letter written at Hampstead on 4th August 1821 to Fisher, in which Constable says, "–at this place I have sundry small works going on–for which purpose I have cleared a small shed in the garden, which held sand, coals, mops and brooms and that is literally a coal hole, and have made it a workshop, and a place of refuge when I am down from the house. I have done a good deal of work here."

The reference to Peel in the inscription on the stretcher remains unexplained, although he would appear to have been the owner when the sketch appeared as lot 5 in an untraced sale on February 18th 1848.

23 Study of Tree Trunks

(?) c. 1821-2. Oil on paper, $9\frac{3}{4} \times 11\frac{1}{2}$ inches ($24\cdot8 \times 29\cdot2$ cm.), London, Victoria and Albert Museum, No. 323–1888 (Isabel Constable Bequest).

Literature: C. J. Holmes, *Constable and his Influence on Landscape Painting*, London, 1902, p. 249 (dated 1830).

Graham Reynolds, *Catalogue of the Constable Collection in the Victoria and Albert Museum*, London, 1960, p. 141, No. 234, Pl. 178.

Reproduced: C. J. Holmes, *Constable*, London, 1901, Pl. XXI.

C. R. Leslie, *Memoirs of the Life of John Constable R.A.*, ed. Jonathan Mayne, London, 1951, p. 416, Pl. 46.

This sketch is a pure essay in light and colour. Constable did not possess Turner's range or his visionary strength, yet his intensity of feeling for nature empowered him to produce work in which the associations of natural objects were lost in their essence.

Holmes dates No. 23, 1830. Graham Reynolds, however, places it c. 1821, on the basis of its naturalistic colouring, and the absence of any trace of the palette knife. He further compares the freedom of the brushwork in the drawing of the foliage with No. 15, *Study of Sky and Trees at Hampstead*.

24 Study of Clouds

1822, September 5. Oil on paper, $11\frac{3}{4} \times 19$ inches ($29\cdot8 \times 48\cdot3$ cm.), London, Victoria and Albert Museum, No. 590–1888 (Isabel Constable Bequest).

Inscribed on the back in ink by the artist *Sepr. 5. 1822. looking S.E. noon. Wind very brisk. & effect bright and fresh. Clouds. moving very fast. with occasional very bright openings to the blue.*

There is also a child's pencil drawing of a house on the back. This is inscribed in ink by the artist *Drawn by John. Augst–1822.* The inscription would appear to refer to John Charles, the artist's eldest son, who was born in December 1817, and who would have been four years old when he made the drawing.

Literature: C. J. Holmes, *Constable and his Influence on Landscape Painting*, London, 1902, p. 246, (dated 1822).
Kurt Badt, *John Constable's Clouds*, London, 1950, pp. 50-62.
Graham Reynolds, *Catalogue of the Constable Collection in the Victoria and Albert Museum*, London, 1960, p. 149, No. 249, Pl. 188.

This sketch is one of about fifty pure sky studies painted in 1822. As a corpus, the group provides a key to a substantial understanding of Constable's artistic purpose.

His preoccupation with clouds was not just the result of a miller's 'weather eye', nor did it stem entirely from a need to improve the aerial composition in his large pictures, although this was his stated objective. A synthesis of his artistic, philosophic and religious experience manifests itself in these studies in which the phaenomenon of light filtered through clouds is examined with a view to controlling the mood of his landscapes. At this time, the laws of evaporation and precipitation, of warm and cold fronts and barometric pressure concerned the poet, philosopher and artist as much as the scientist. In fact the science of meteorology was in its infancy when Luke Howard first published his classification of cloud formations in *The Climate of London* (1818), but the subject was perfectly understood by Shelley in his poem *The Cloud* (1820), and Goethe saw in meteorology a symbol of the universal law. He placed it among the 'elemental and original relationships which belong both to the human intellect and to nature'.

25 Study of Cirrus Clouds

c. 1822. Oil on paper, $4\frac{1}{2} \times 7$ inches ($11 \cdot 4 \times 17 \cdot 8$ cm.), London, Victoria and Albert Museum, No. 784–1888 (Isabel Constable Bequest).

Inscribed on the back in ink *Painted by John Constable R.A.*, over an earlier inscription (nearly illegible), which appears to have been written by the artist and perhaps reads *cirrus*.

Exhibited: Tate Gallery, *Centenary Exhibition of Paintings and Watercolours by John Constable R.A.*, 1937, No. 124 (a).

Literature: C. J. Holmes, *Constable*, London, 1901, p. 19.
C. J. Holmes, *Constable and his Influence on Landscape Painting*, London, 1902, p. 245, (dated 1821).
Kurt Badt, *John Constable's Clouds*, London, 1950, pp. 50 and 51.
C. R. Leslie, *Memoirs of the Life of John Constable R.A.*, ed. Jonathan Mayne, London, 1951, p. 161, Pl. VIII.
Graham Reynolds, *Catalogue of the Constable Collection in the Victoria and Albert Museum*, London, 1960, p. 149, No. 250, Pl. 189.

This sketch gives an excellent impression of the texture of the feathery ice cloud. The obscure inscription on the back, if it does indeed read 'cirrus', would indicate that Constable was familiar with Luke Howard's terminology.

Unlike No. 24, *Study of Clouds,* this sketch does not bear notes on the weather conditions and a date. Those of Constable's fifty or so pure cloud studies which are dated show that they were nearly all executed in August and September 1822. In October 1822, Constable wrote to Fisher complaining that his stay at Hampstead had cost him time, insofar that he needed money for his move from Keppel Street to Charlotte Street, and work on his commissions was falling behind.

Although they were undertaken as a means to an end; as working studies to develop the feeling for aerial space and light in his finished compositions, the sky studies were never surpassed. Particularly in the skies of his later work, Constable failed to recapture the unforced, natural quality of these sketches.

26 Study of Houses amidst Trees: Evening

1823, October 4th. Oil on paper, $9\frac{7}{8} \times 12\frac{1}{8}$ inches (25·1 × 30·7 cm.), London, Victoria and Albert Museum, No. 152–1888 (Isabel Constable Bequest).

Inscribed on the back in pencil by the artist *Saturday Evg 4th Oct 1823.*

Exhibited: Tate Gallery, *Centenary Exhibition of Paintings and Watercolours by John Constable R.A.*, 1937, No. 118 (b).

Literature: C. J. Holmes, *Constable and his Influence on Landscape Painting*, London, 1902, p. 246, (dated 1823).
C. R. Leslie, *Memoirs of the Life of John Constable R.A.*, ed. Jonathan Mayne, London, 1951, p. 414. Pl. 34.
Graham Reynolds, *Catalogue of the Constable Collection in the Victoria and Albert Museum*, London, 1960, p. 161, No. 258, Pl. 198.

Constable settled his family at Stamford Lodge, Hampstead, during the summer and autumn of 1823. He visited them in June and early August but went to stay with Fisher at Salisbury and Gillingham from the 19th August until well into September. Somewhat conscience stricken about his long absence from his wife–"My visit has been as pleasant as it could be without you and my darlings–but not over comfortable on this account", Constable returned to Hampstead only to accept an invitation to stay with Sir George Beaumont at Coleorton Hall in Leicestershire for the latter part of October and November.

It is odd that at a period when Constable was painting some of his most beautiful small sketches, we find him in his letters grudging the time spent away from full size canvases. Writing on the 30th September 1823 to thank Fisher for the visit to Gillingham, Constable says "I found my wife and children all well, better than I have ever had them–since they belonged to me. They wish for a little longer stay at Hampstead– but (it) sadly unsettles me–to be torn away from my painting room– and the work I do up there by littles is of no avail. I am now pretty full handed–I have several pretty minor things to do–but my difficulty lies in what I am to do for the world, next year. I must work for myself–and must have a large canvas". In his next letter to Fisher, dated 19th October 1823, he says, "I want to get to my easil in Town–and not to witness (the) rotting melancholy dissolution of the trees etc.,–which two months ago were so beautiful–and lovely". Constable's impatience to get on with large canvases may have partly been his wish as breadwinner for his family to produce work that would bring in money. After his father-in-law's death, the Constables received a considerable legacy which prompted him to write, "I shall now stand before a six foot canvas with a mind at ease (thank God)".

Constable had always declared that the freshness of spring inspired him more than autumnal tints, yet he frequently achieved, as in the present instance, beautiful effects with the soft light of a late autumn afternoon. The sketch appears to have been made in the vicinity of Hampstead.

27 Brighton Beach

1824, June 12th. Oil on paper, $4\frac{3}{4} \times 11\frac{5}{8}$ inches ($12 \times 29 \cdot 7$ cm.), London, Victoria and Albert Museum, No. 783–1888 (Isabel Constable Bequest).
Inscribed on the back in pencil by the artist *June 12 1824*, and in another hand with deletions *taking the air – Squaly day*.

Exhibited: Tate Gallery, *Centenary Exhibition of Paintings and Watercolours by John Constable R.A.*, 1937, No. 128 (a).

Literature: C. J. Holmes, *Constable and his Influence on Landscape Painting*, London, 1902, p. 246, (dated 1824).
Graham Reynolds, *Catalogue of the Constable Collection in the Victoria and Albert Museum*, London, 1960, p. 164, No. 264, Pl. 200.

Reproduced: E. V. Lucas, *John Constable the Painter*, London, 1924, Pl. 15.

Constable established his wife and family at Brighton for the first time in May 1824. He visited them intermittantly until August, sketching while he was there. Mrs. Constable was already showing signs of the illness which was to prove fatal four years later, and the sea air was intended as a tonic. One is led to wonder whether Constable was already aware that her symptoms betrayed the fact that she was suffering from the then dreaded disease of pulmonary tuberculosis.

There is a sad reflective note in this lonely scene with its subtle, overcast sky and sense of failing light. The simple composition is perfectly balanced by the barge, which is silently passing out of the picture in the opposite direction from the walkers. On the 29th August 1824 Constable wrote to Fisher, "–there is nothing here for a painter but the breakers and sky–which have been lovely indeed and always varying".

28 Brighton Beach, with Colliers

1824, July 19. Oil on paper, $5\frac{7}{8} \times 9\frac{3}{4}$ inches ($14 \cdot 9 \times 24 \cdot 8$ cm.), London, Victoria and Albert Museum, No. 591–1888 (Isabel Constable Bequest).

Inscribed on the back in pencil, (probably by the artist, but partly copied in ink, or inked over), *3d tide receeding left the beach wet–Head of the Chain Pier Beach Brighton July 19 Evg., 1824. My dear Maria's Birthday Your Goddaughter–Very lovely Evening–looking Eastward–cliffs and light off a dark grey (?) effect–background–very white and golden light*. Inscribed with the monogram *JC*. Also inscribed in ink over an earlier pencil inscription *Colliers on the beach*. Maria Louisa Constable was Fisher's god-daughter.

Exhibited: Tate Gallery, *Centenary Exhibition of Paintings and Watercolours by John Constable R.A.*, 1937, No. 115 (a).
Paris, Palais du Louvre, *La Peinture Anglaise XVIIIe et XIXe Siècles*, 1938, No. 24.

Literature: C. J. Holmes, *Constable*, London, 1901, p. 19, Pl. XV.
C. J. Holmes, *Constable and his Influence on Landscape Painting*, London, 1902, p. 246, (dated 1824).
C. R. Leslie, *Memoirs of the Life of John Constable R.A.*, ed. Jonathan Mayne, London, 1951, pp. 136 and 413, Pl. 32.
Graham Reynolds, *Catalogue of the Constable Collection in the Victoria and Albert Museum*, p. 164, No. 266, Pl. 202.

Reproduced: E. V. Lucas, *John Constable the Painter*, London, 1924, Pl. 14.

74

Constable has achieved a remarkable sense of atmosphere in this little sketch, which he painted as he sat at the head of the Chain Pier. A warm clear light pervades the whole picture, and there is a gentle breeze filling the white sails of the barges as a fine summer day draws to a close.

Despite his engagements with the Paris dealers, Constable had taken the coach down from London especially to be with his family on his daughter's birthday. The note on the back of the sketch, although it conforms with his customary remarks about prevailing conditions of light, weather, etc., is clearly addressed to Fisher, because it refers to *My dear Maria's Birthday Your Goddaughter*. John Fisher was god-father to Maria Louisa, Constable's eldest daughter, then just aged five.

It would seem likely that, with perhaps No. 27, *Brighton Beach* and No. 29, *A Windmill near Brighton*, it was among a group of sketches which Constable lent to Fisher. Referring to them in a letter of the 5th January 1825, addressed to Fisher, he says, "I have enclosed in the box a dozen of my oil sketches–perhaps the sight of the sea may cheer Mrs. F(isher)– they were done in the lid of my box on my knees as usual!" Fisher returned them three months later, together with two volumes of Paley's sermons which, he said, "are fit companions for your sketches, being exactly like them: full of vigour, and mature, fresh, original, warm from observation of nature, hasty, unpolished, untouched afterwards."

29 A Windmill near Brighton

1824, August 3. Oil on paper, $6\frac{3}{8} \times 12\frac{1}{8}$ inches ($16\cdot2 \times 30\cdot8$ cm.), London, Victoria and Albert Museum, No. 149–1888 (Isabel Constable Bequest).

Inscribed on the back in pencil by the artist, *Brighton Augst. 3ᵈ 1824 Smock or Tower Mill west end of Brighton the neighbourhood of Brighton – consists of London cow fields – and Hideous masses of unfledged earth called the country.*

Exhibited: Tate Gallery, *Centenary Exhibition of Paintings and Watercolours by John Constable R.A.*, 1937, No. 113 (b).
Manchester City Art Gallery, *John Constable*, 1956, No. 61.

Literature: C. J. Holmes, *Constable and his Influence on Landscape Painting*, London, 1902, p. 246, (dated 1824).
Graham Reynolds, *Catalogue of Constable Collection in the Victoria and Albert Museum*, London, 1960, p. 165, No. 268, Pl. 204.

Despite the beauty of his Brighton sketches, Constable always expressed a strong distaste for the place. Apart from his unflattering description on the back of this sketch, he wrote to Fisher on the 29th August 1824, "Brighton is the receptacle of fashion and off-scouring of London. The magnificence of the sea, and its (to use your own beautiful expression) 'everlasting voice', is drowned in the din and lost in the tumult of stage coaches, gigs, 'flys' etc., and the beach is only Piccadilly, – by the seaside. Ladies dressed and *undressed;* gentlemen in morning gowns and slippers on, or without them altogether about *knee deep* in the breakers – footmen, children, nursery-maids, dogs, boys, fishermen and Preventive Service men (with hangers and pistols); rotten fish, and those hideous amphibious animals, the old bathing-women, whose language, both in oaths and voice, resembles men, all mixed together in endless and indecent confusion." Constable's description, although he didn't paint these Frithlike scenes, appears to betray a certain fascination with them.

30 Coast Scene, perhaps at Brighton: Evening

(?) 1828, May 22nd. Oil on paper, $7\frac{7}{8} \times 9\frac{3}{4}$ inches ($20 \times 24 \cdot 8$ cm.), London, Victoria and Albert Museum, No. 155–1888 (Isabel Constable Bequest).

Inscribed on the back in pencil by the artist *22 May*. Also on the back, a rough scribble in pencil and oil and the monogram *JC*.

Exhibited: Tate Gallery, *Centenary Exhibition of Paintings and Watercolours by John Constable R.A.*, 1937, No. 108 (b).

Literature: C. J. Holmes, *Constable and his Influence on Landscape Painting*, London, 1902, p. 247, (dated 1824).
Graham Reynolds, *Catalogue of the Constable Collection in the Victoria and Albert Museum*, London, 1960, p. 183, No. 303, Pl. 228.

Reproduced: E. V. Lucas, *Constable the Painter*, London, 1924, Pl. 27.

Constable has inscribed the date *22 May* on the back of this sketch. He is known, on the evidence of dated pencil sketches in the Victoria and Albert Museum to have been at Brighton on the 16th and on the 30th May, 1828. Further, the scene was identified as being possibly at Brighton at the time it was received into the Victoria and Albert Museum in 1888. On this basis Graham Reynolds dates the sketch 1828? May 22.

Constable went to Brighton in May to collect those children who had not been taken to London the previous month. His father-in-law, Charles Bicknell, had died in March, and Maria Constable was staying at the Bicknell's cottage at Putney. Maria's health was now so bad that it did not permit her being moved. Constable reported in a note to Samuel Lane, "My poor wife is still very ill at Putney, and when I can get her home I know not. We talk of Brighton, but we only talk of it. She can't make such a journey."

Like No. 16 *(?) 'The Salt Box', Hampstead*, No. 30 was executed in the late afternoon, and the paint has similarly been laid on a soft pink ground to give an added impression of warmth to the overall tone.

31 Hampstead after a Thunderstorm

1830. Oil on paper laid on panel, $6\frac{1}{8} \times 7\frac{5}{8}$ inches (15·5 × 19·5 cm.), Upperville, Virginia, Mr. and Mrs. Paul Mellon, No. 62/3/15/11.

A label signed by George Constable and transferred from the back of the original panel to a back board reads *Sketch at Hampstead/by/John Constable R.A./ 1830*.

Collections: George Constable.
                I. R. Lilburn.

Exhibited: Museum of Fine Arts, Richmond, Virginia, *Painting in England 1700-1850*, 1963, No. 103, Pl. 32.
                Royal Academy, London, *Painting in England 1700-1850*, 1964-5, No. 72.

There is a noticeable reduction in the output of oil sketches towards the end of Constable's life. This was in part due to the fact that much of his time went into supervising the *English Landscape* series of mezzotints.

The present scene may represent the path now called Judge's Walk looking towards Windmill Hill. The disturbed, nervous handling of the paint and the dramatic, threatening sky became a characteristic of Constable's later work, and was a reflection of his increasing moroseness and depressed state of mind. His wife, who had died two years earlier, had always been a stablising element in his turbulent nature. Her practical kindness and steady, if undemonstrative affection are everywhere evident in her letters to him. The effect on such a sensitive mind as his, of watching her slowly waste away and die, must have added greatly to the sense of injustice which had always been latent in him. His parents and his wife had been loving and kind, and despite having had to live frugally at times, he had never suffered desperately from material need. The result was that deep misfortune left him with a feeling of persecution and frustration.

32 A View of London, with Sir Richard Steele's Cottage

1832-7. Oil on canvas, $8\frac{1}{4} \times 11\frac{1}{4}$ inches (21×28 cm.), Upperville, Virginia, Mr. and Mrs. Paul Mellon, No. 62/4/19/7.
Engraved by David Lucas and published in 1845.

Collections: Captain C. G. Constable.
                Miss Isabel Constable.
                Thomas James Barrett.
                J. K. Hodgson.
                Sir R. Leicester Harmsworth.
                Sir Geoffrey Harmsworth.

Exhibited: Grosvenor Gallery, London, 1889.
Wildenstein, London, Centenary Exhibition: *John Constable R.A.–his Origins and Influence*, 1937, No. 63.
Manchester City Art Gallery, *John Constable*, 1956, No. 76.
Museum of Fine Arts, Richmond, Virginia, *Painting in England 1700-1850*, 1963, No. 114, Pl. 36.
Royal Academy, London, *Painting in England 1700-1850*, 1964-5, No. 83.

Literature: C. J. Holmes, *Constable and his Influence on Landscape Painting*, London, 1902, p. 250, (the exhibited picture dated 1832).
Andrew Shirley, *The Published Mezzotints of David Lucas after John Constable R.A.*, Oxford, 1930, p. 212, No. 48, Pl. XLVIII.
C. R. Leslie, *Memoirs of the Life of John Constable R.A.*, ed. Andrew Shirley, 1937, p. 285.

The large picture which was exhibited as No. 147, *Sir Richard Steele's Cottage, Hampstead*, at the Royal Academy in 1832 appears to have been lost, but the full-scale sketch for the subject is in the possession of Sir Kenneth Clark. No. 32 was painted as a small replica, presumably intended for David Lucas's use in the preparation of his mezzotint, although the plate was not published until 1845, eight years after Constable's death.

The view is in fact somewhat distorted; something unimaginable in Constable's earlier practice. Sir Richard Steele's cottage was situated at what is now the lower part of Haverstock Hill, at a point from which it was not possible to enjoy a view of London and St. Paul's.

There is little use of the palette knife, and although the style is slightly cramped, this charming sketch does not bear witness to the mannerisms that crept into much of Constable's later work.